Unexpected interior

By Nathaniel D. Lauser

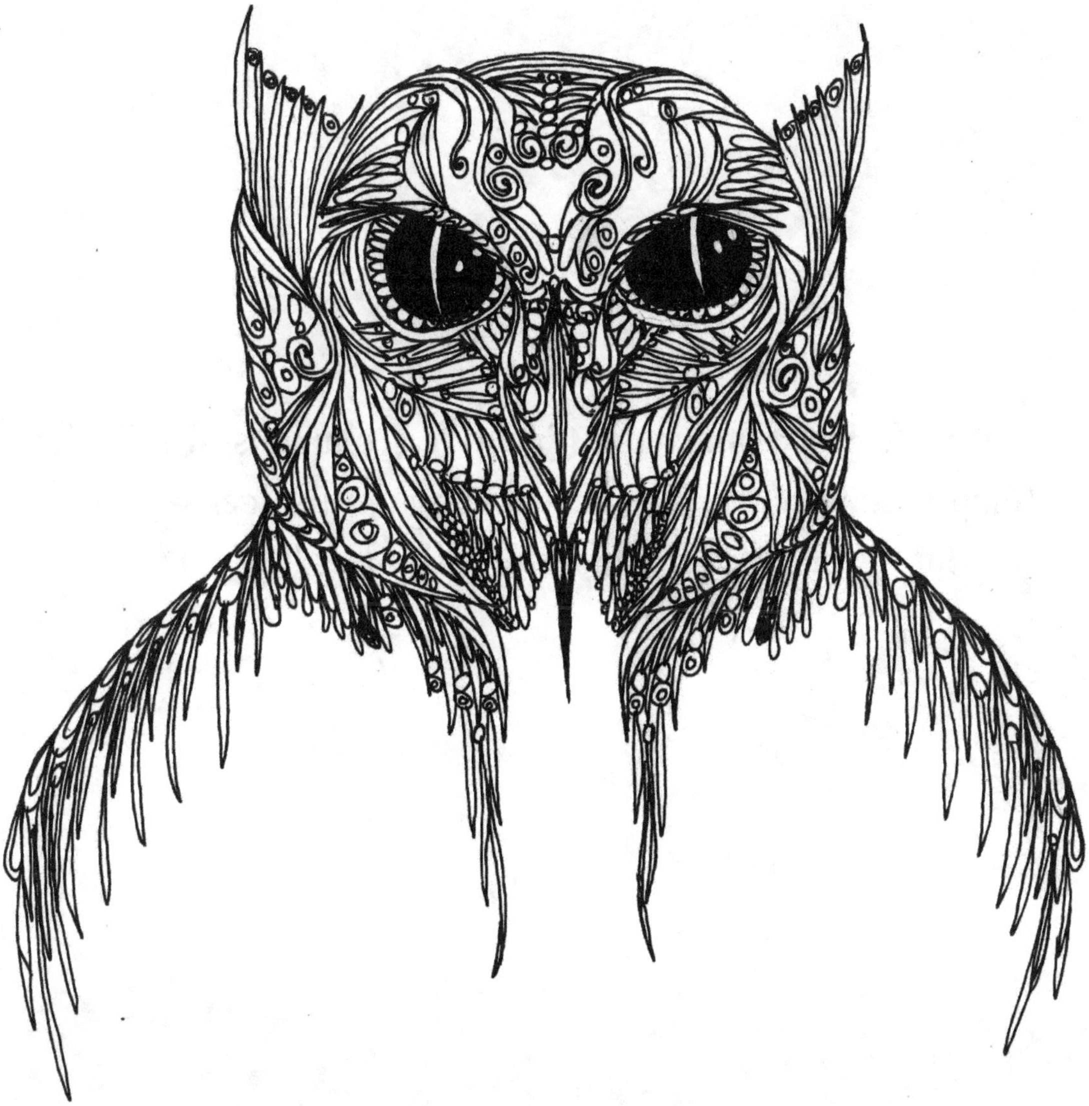

Hall of Contents

I like to use a fine, felt tip pen, a sharp pencil, or a ball point gel pen to color in my pictures.

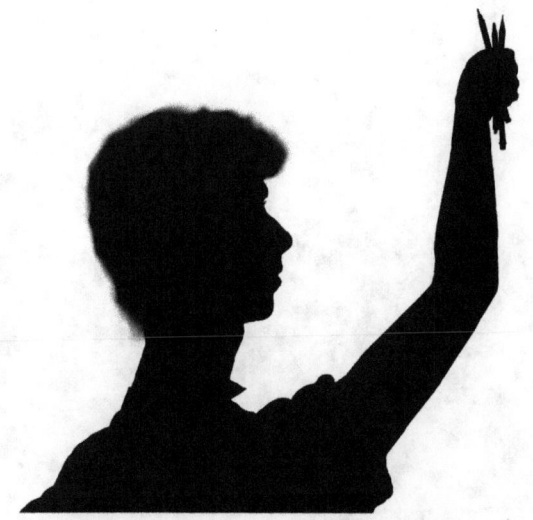

Forward into...

The Realm of Flight

Star

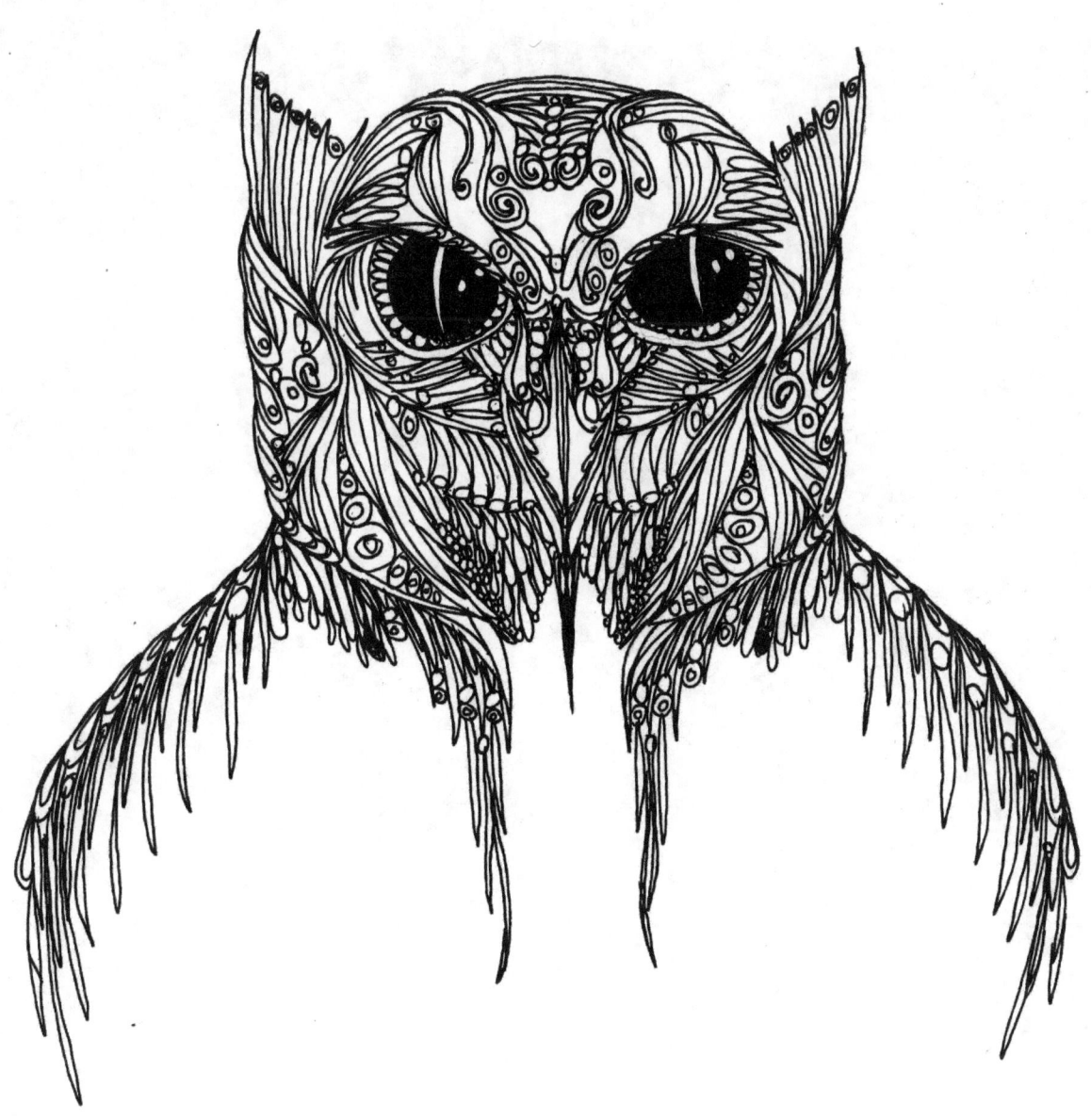

Soar

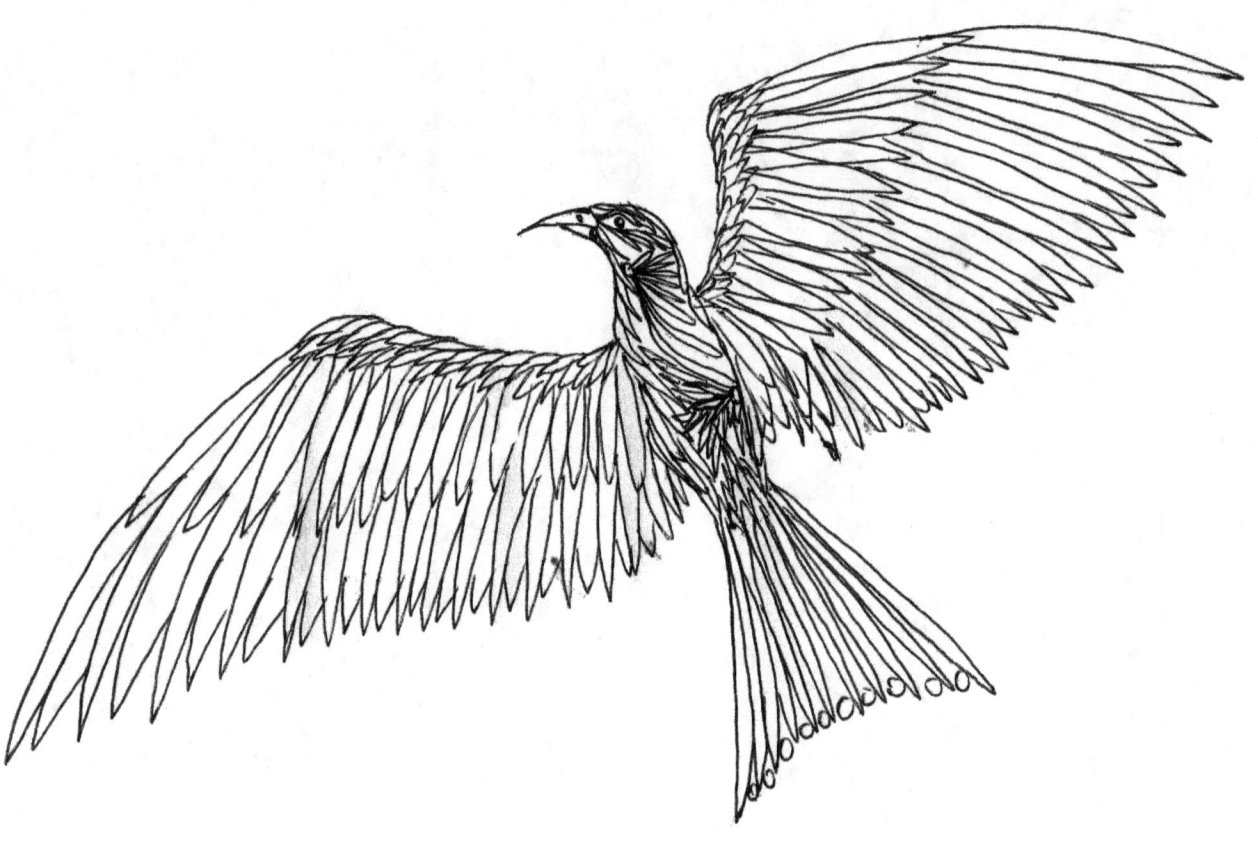

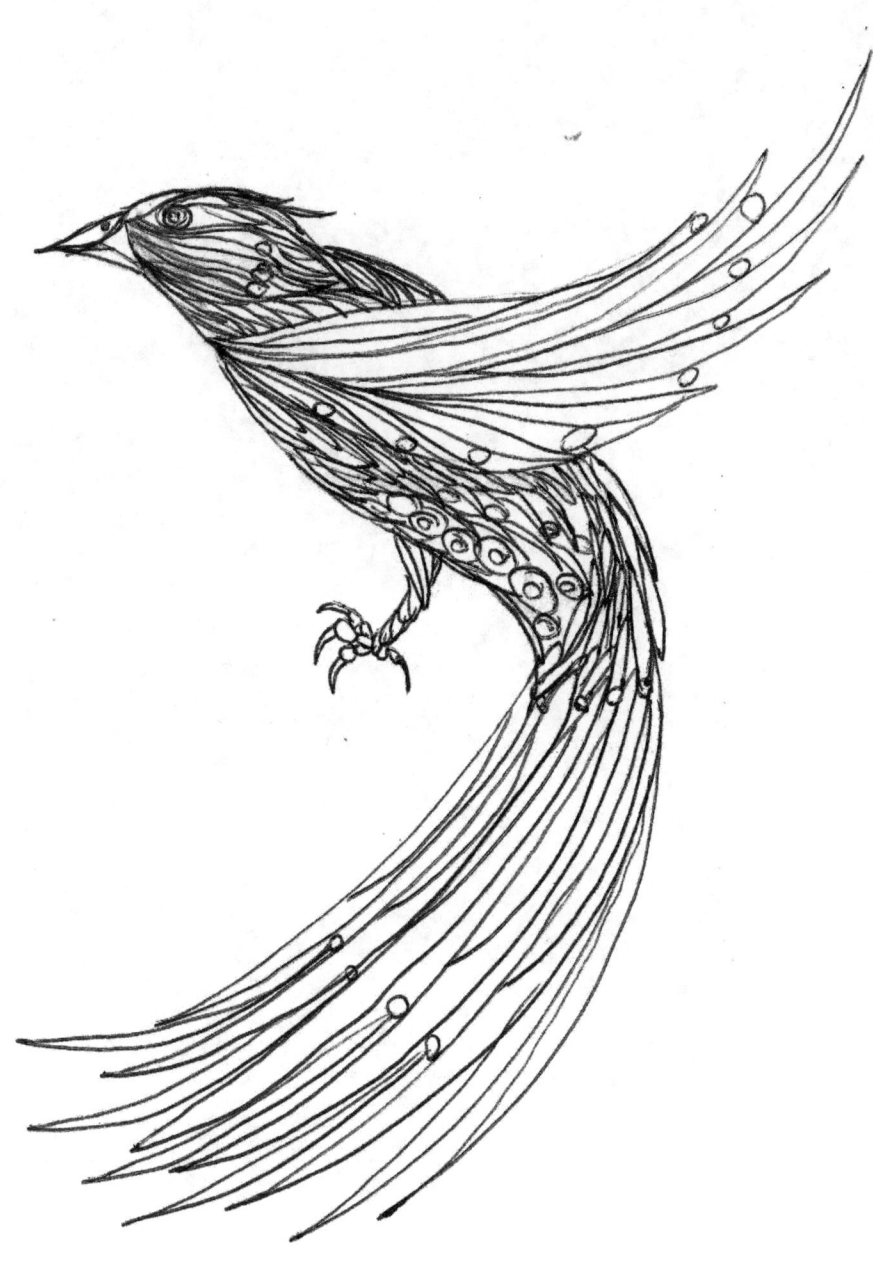

Bloom

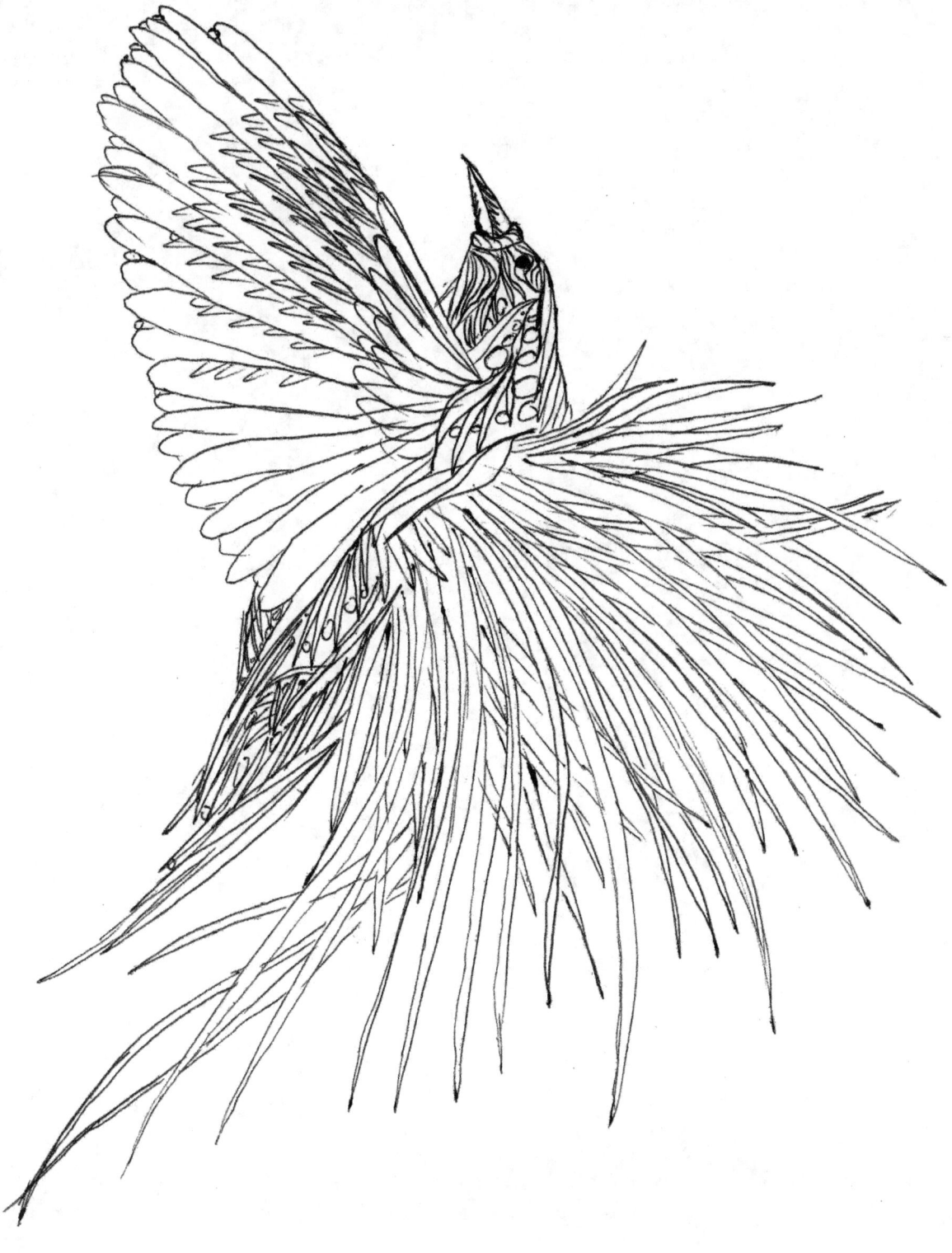

Cape

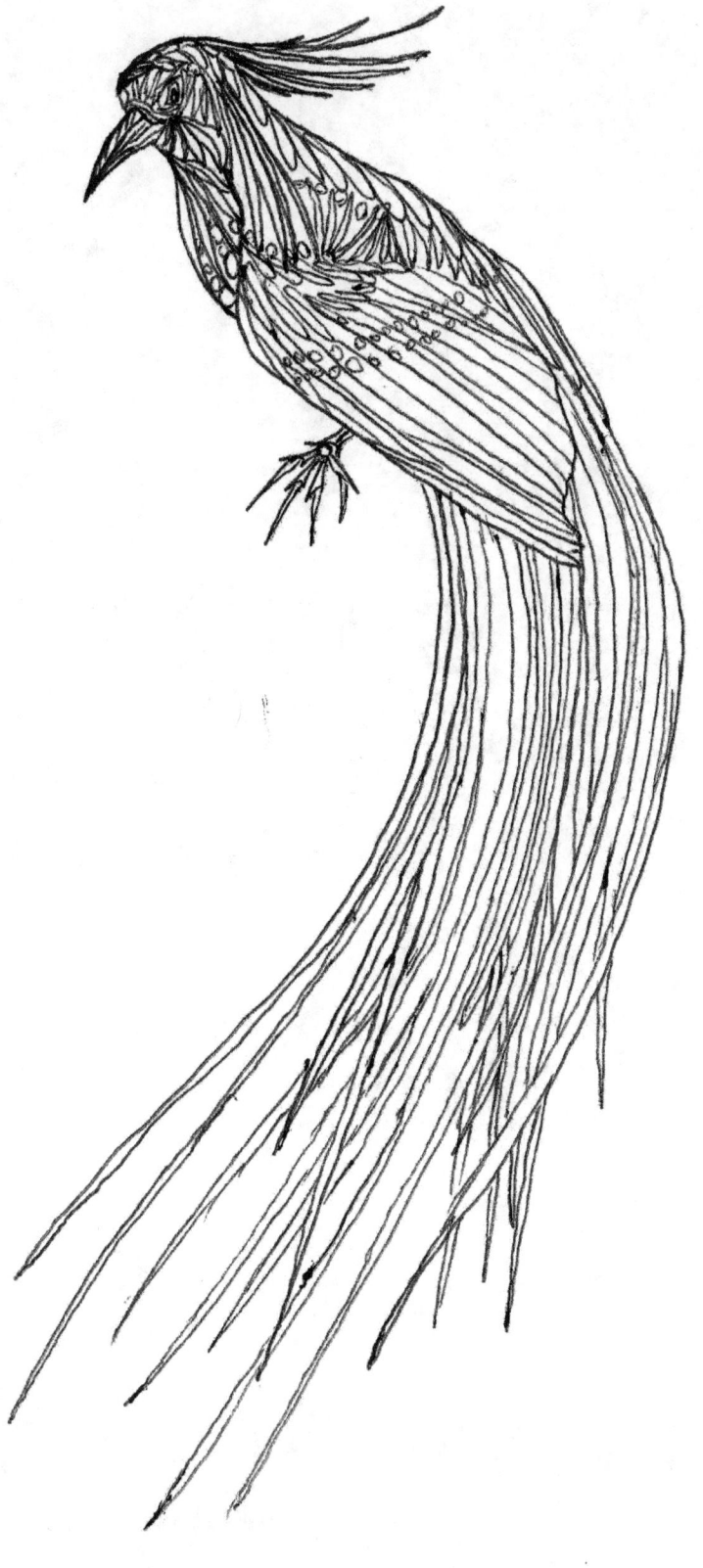

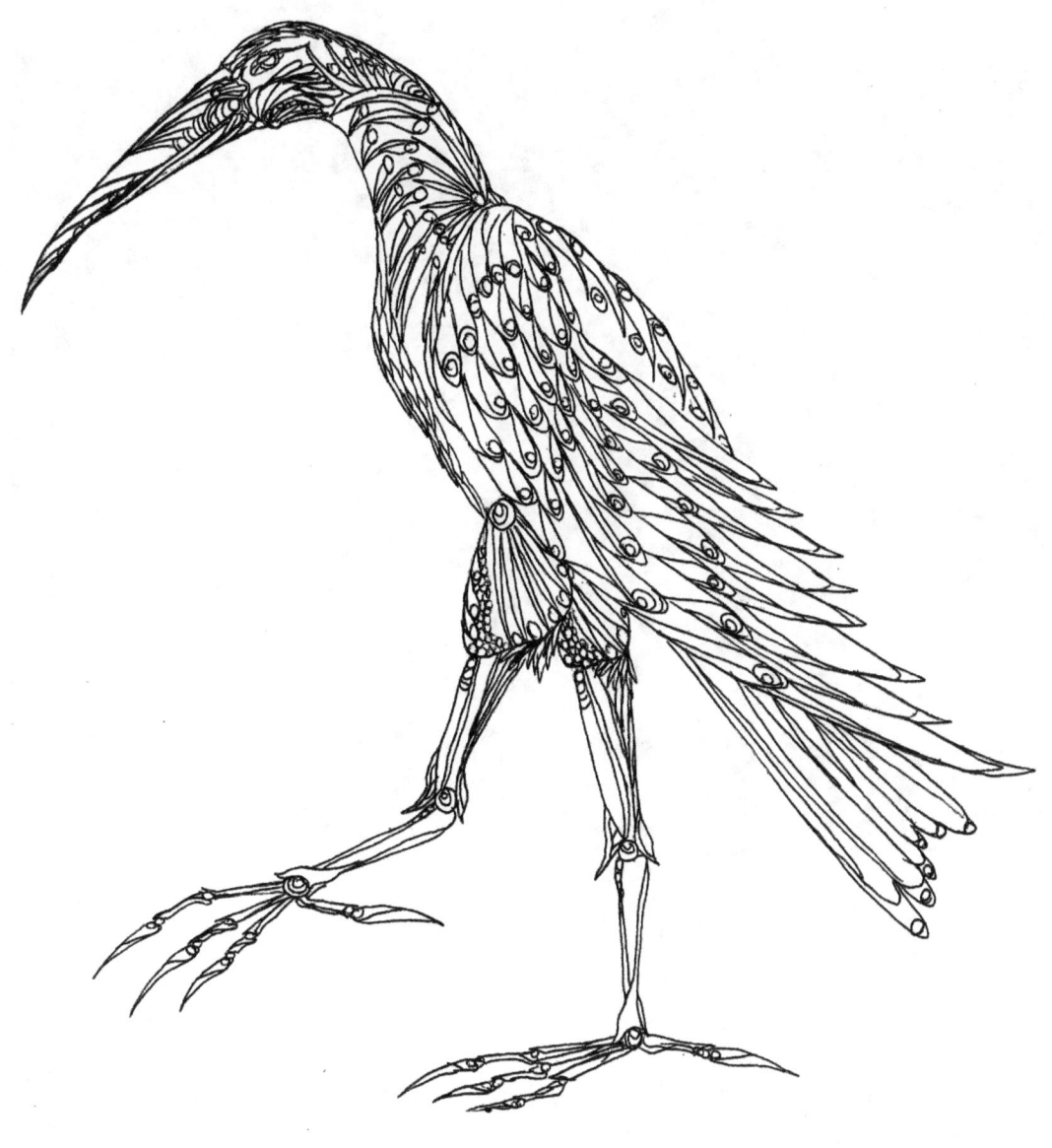

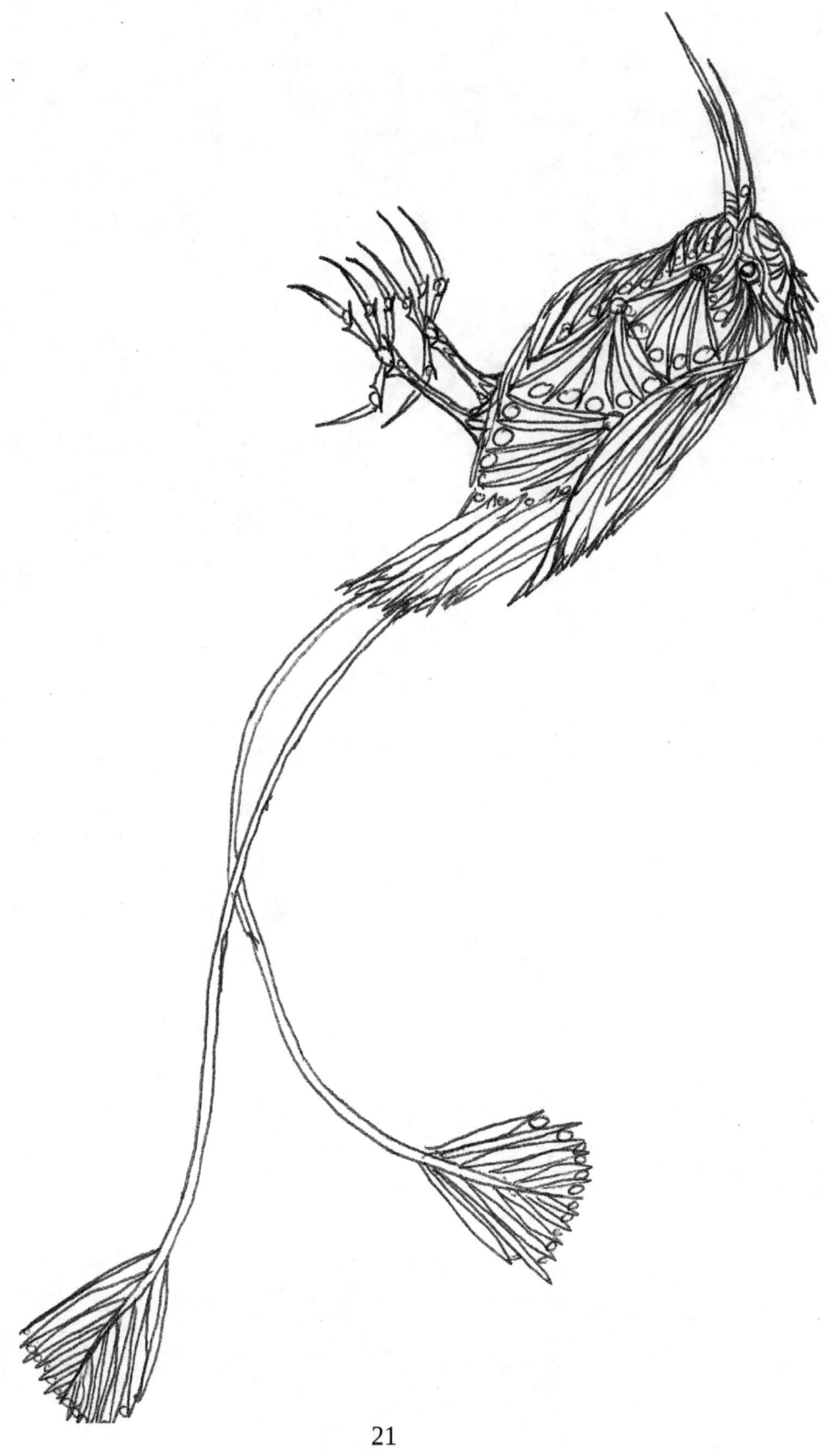

Broad Wing

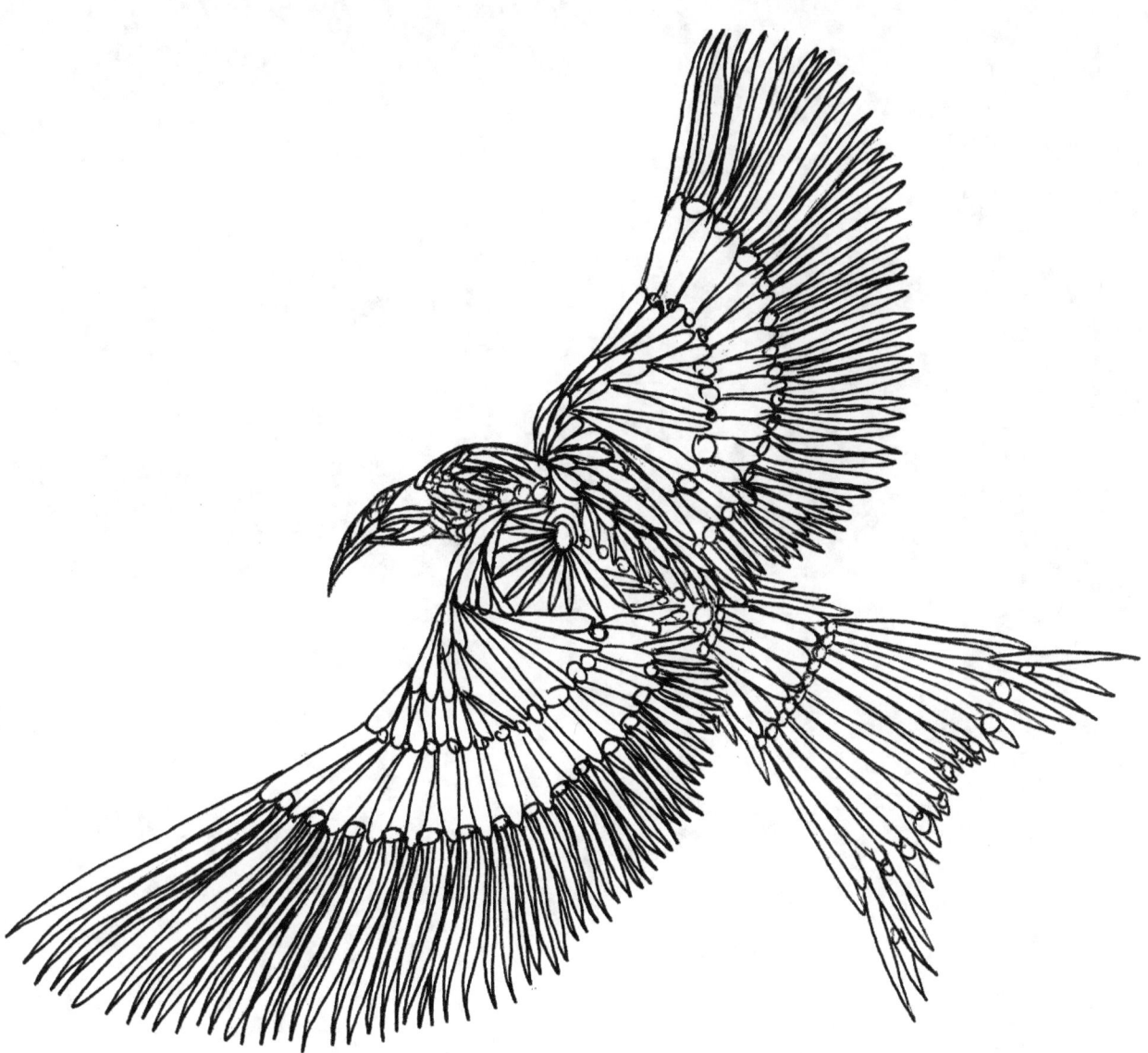

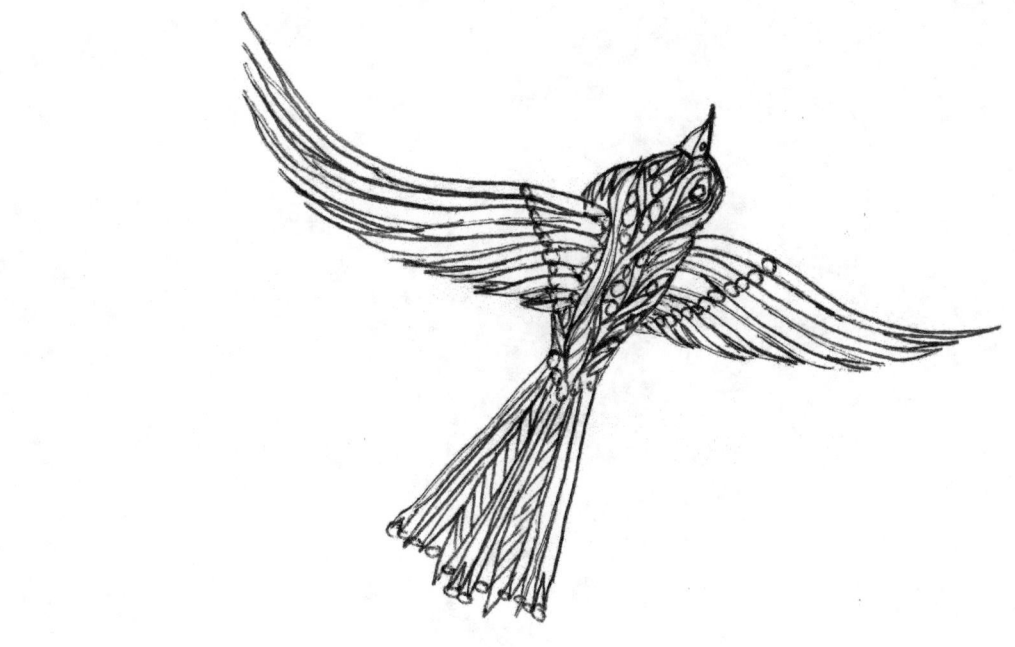

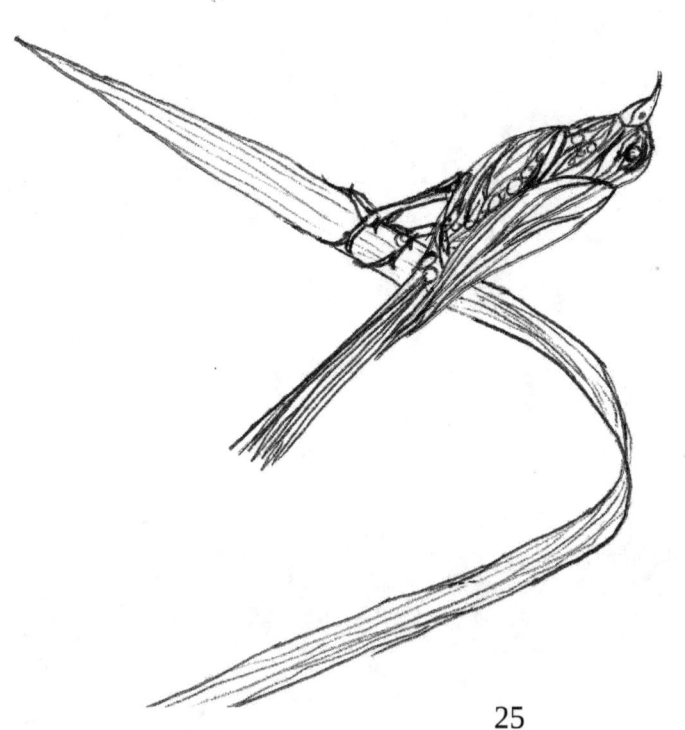

The Realm of the Sea

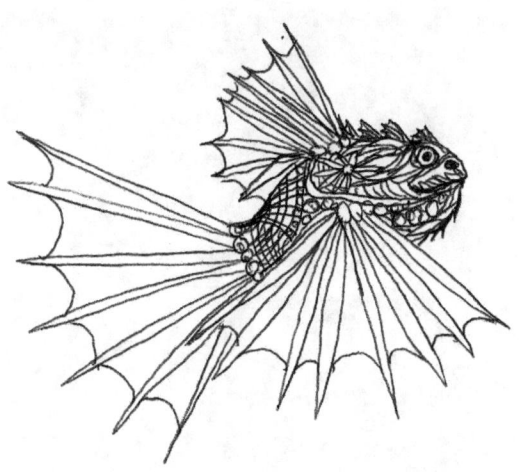

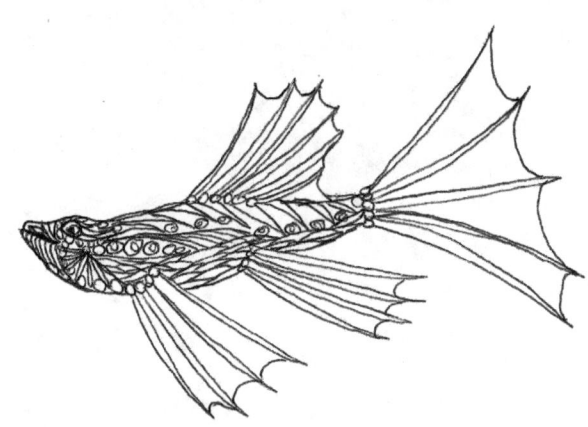

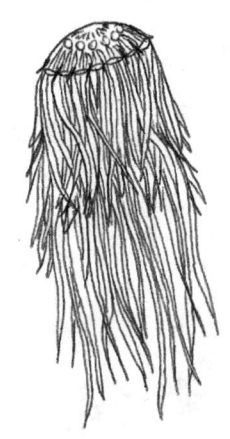

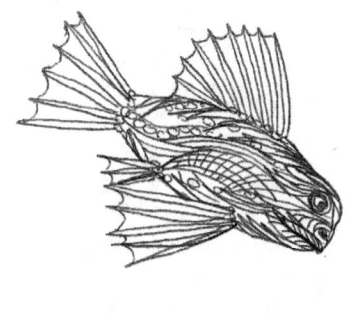

Green Haired Shark

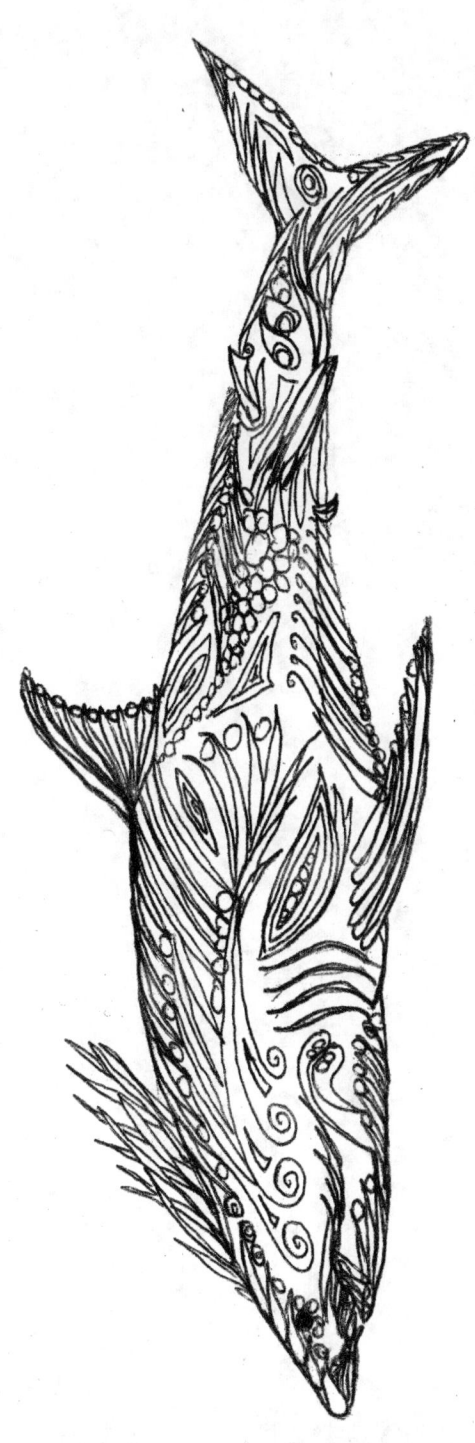

Crawdad

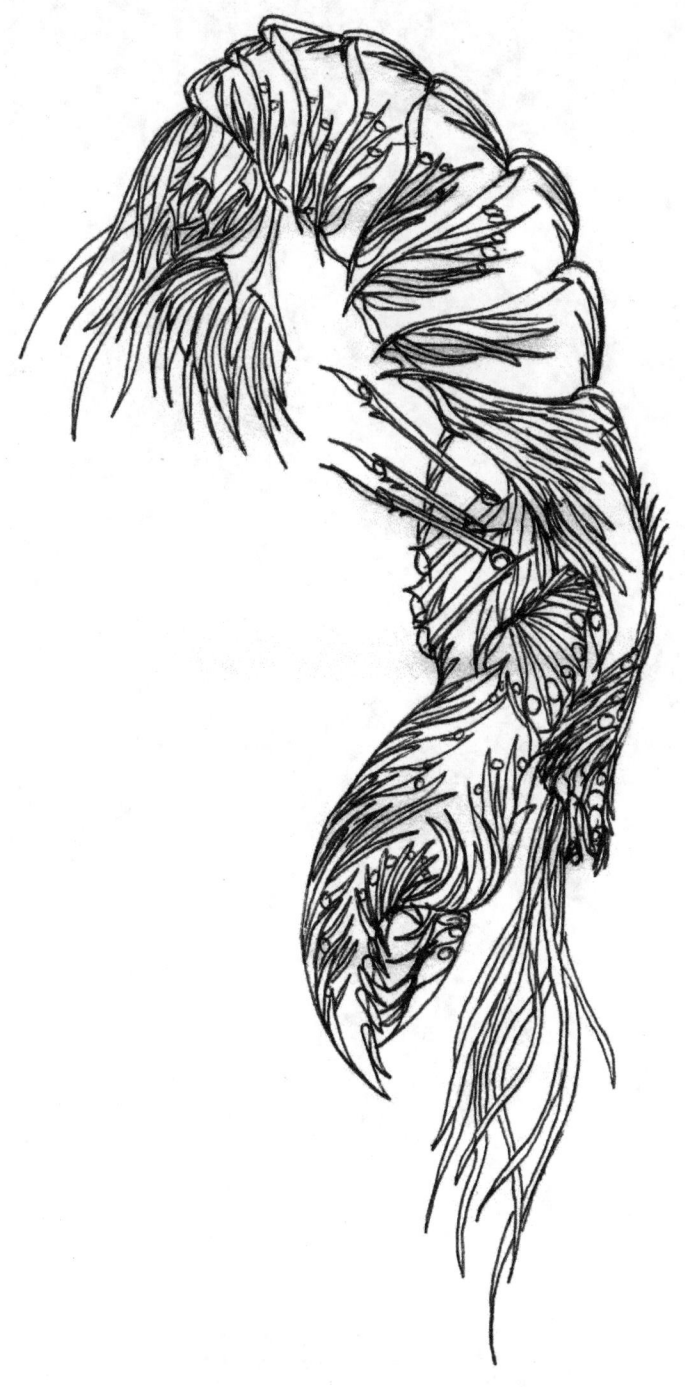

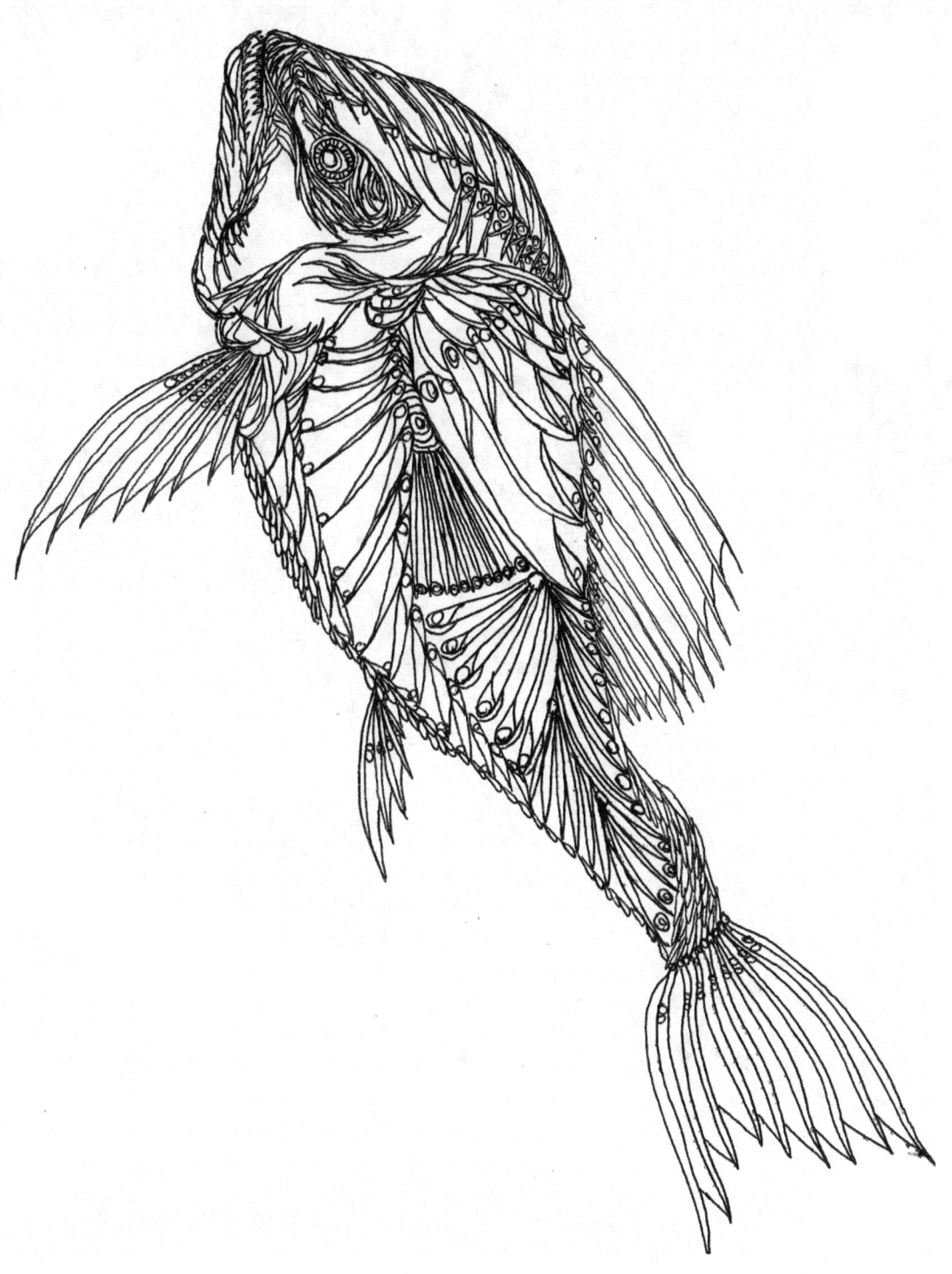

Rumbles

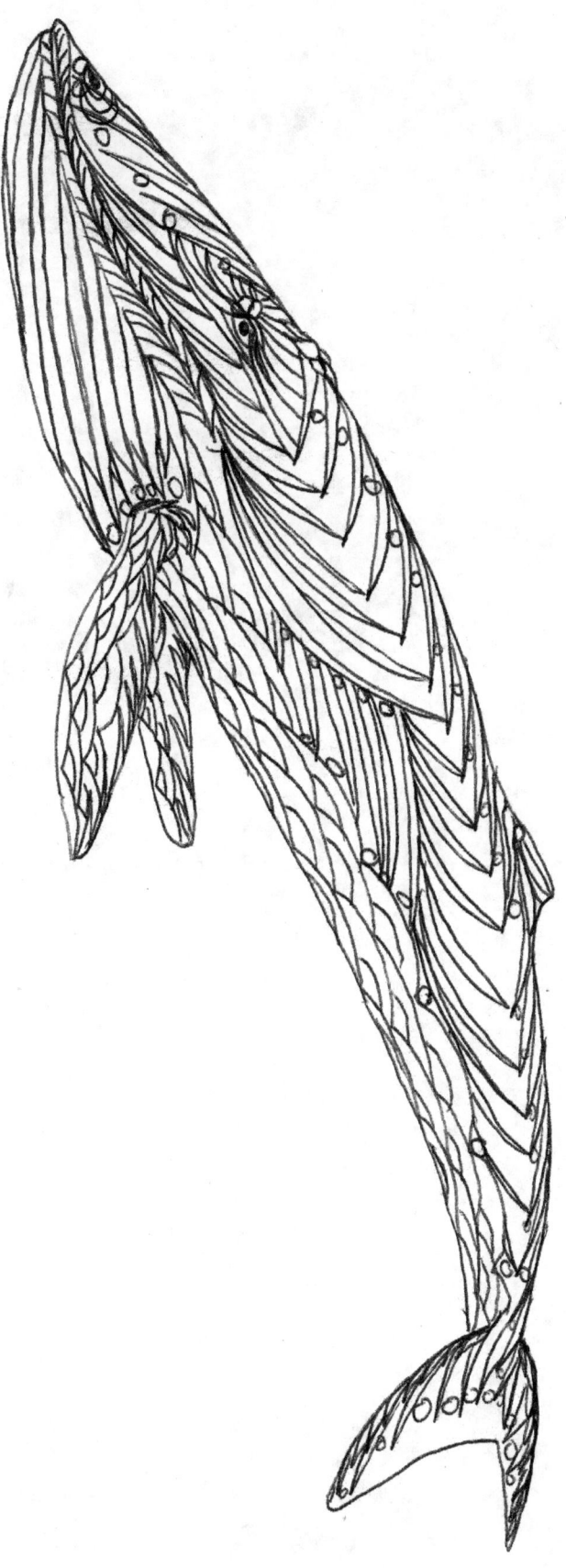

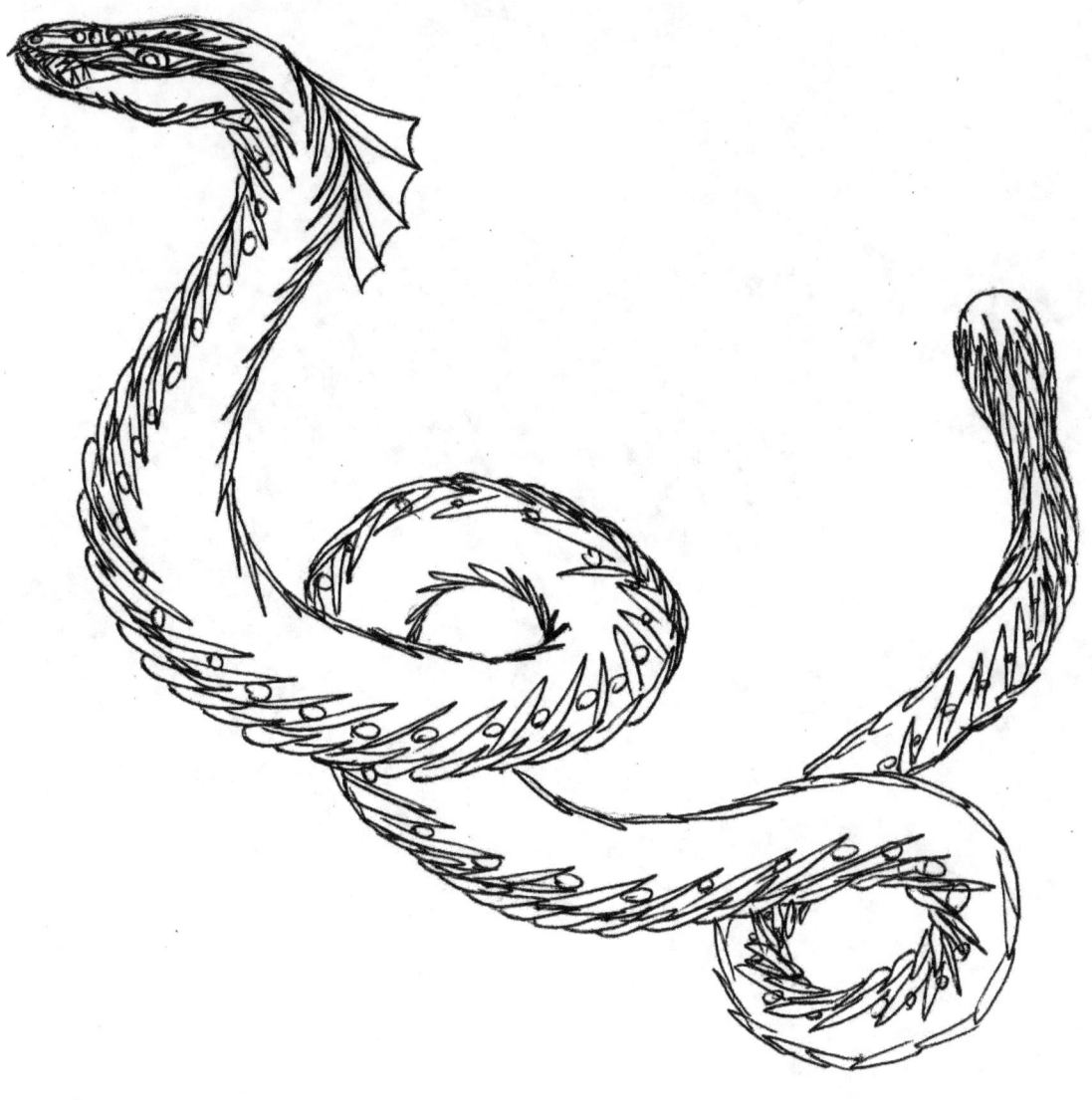

Tadpole

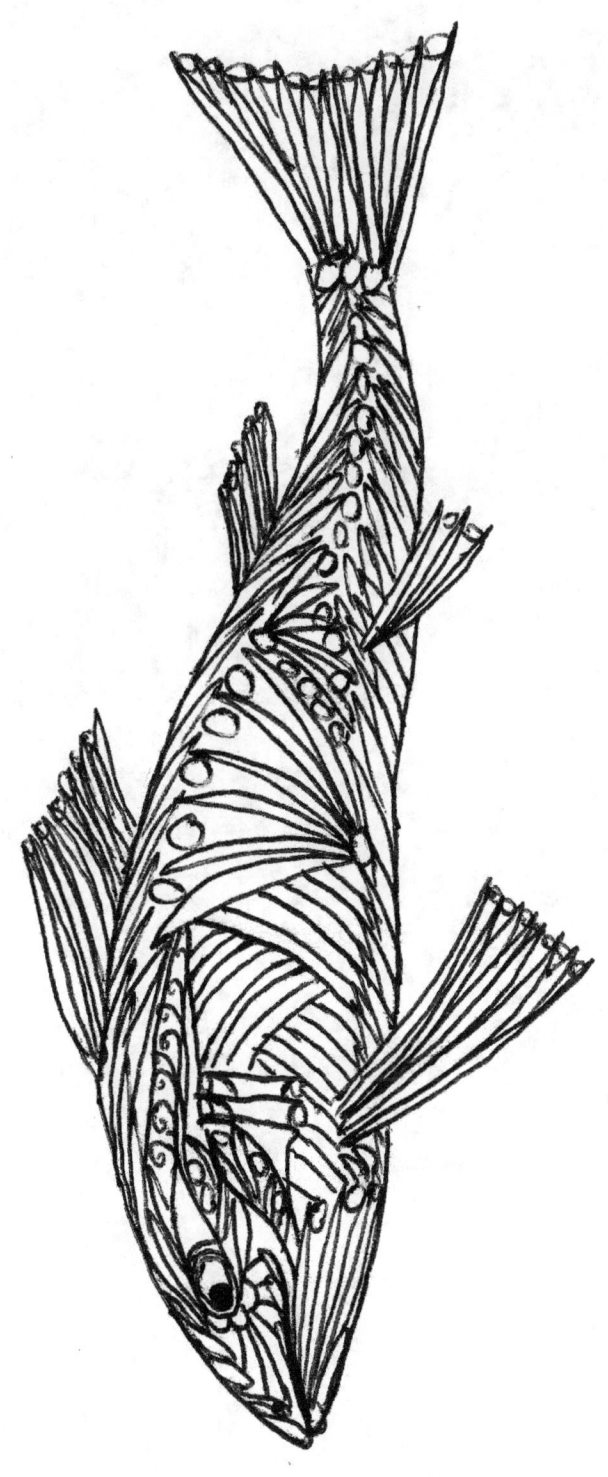

Narwhal

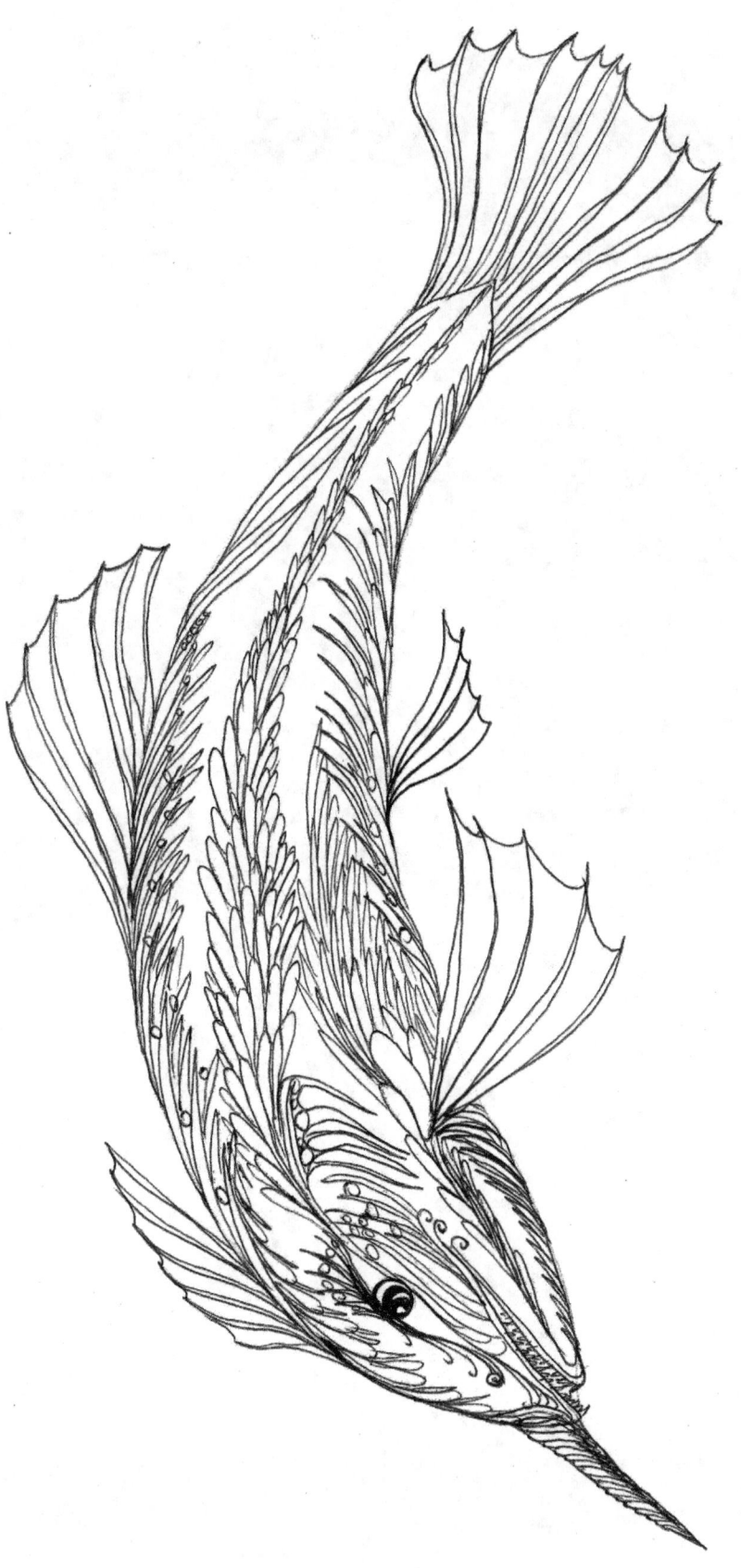

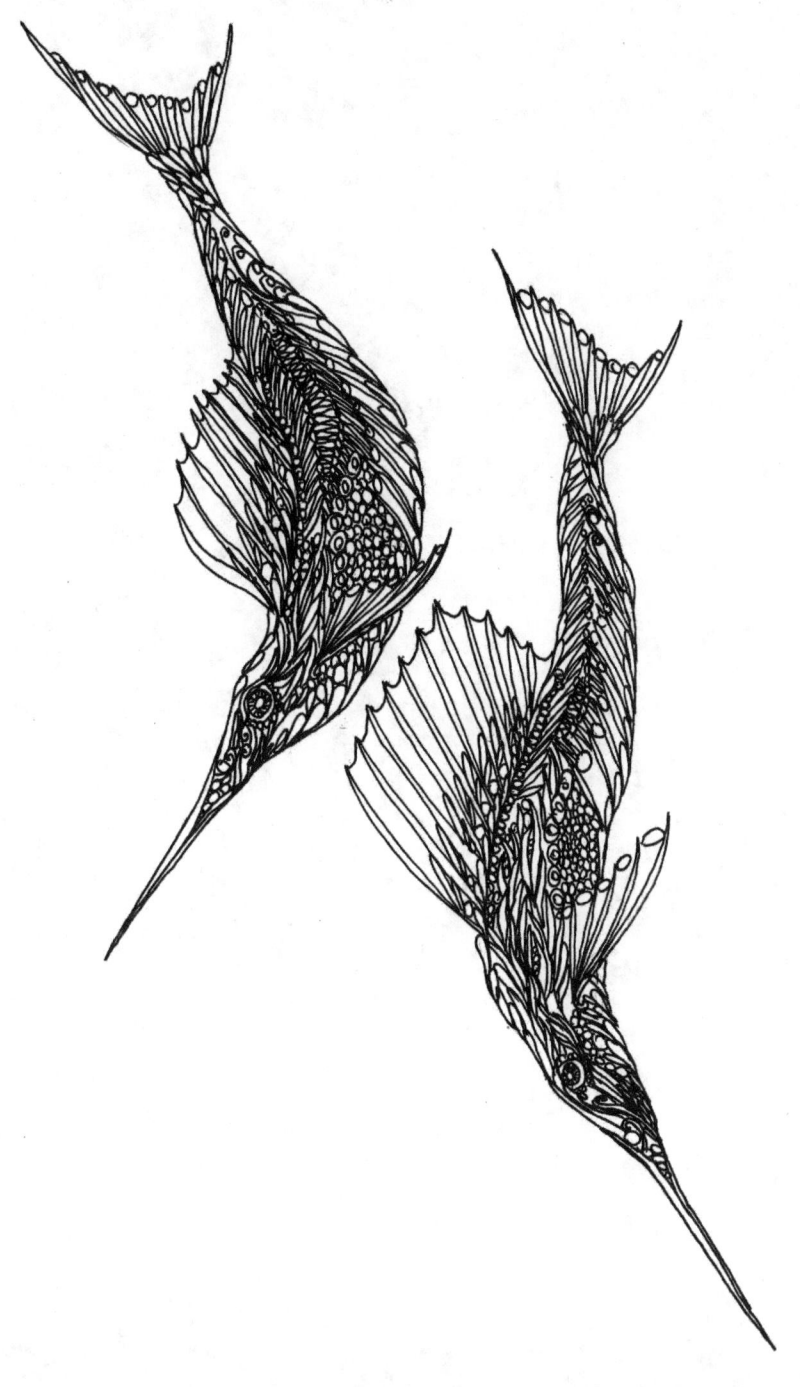

The Realm of Creeping Things

Arachnid

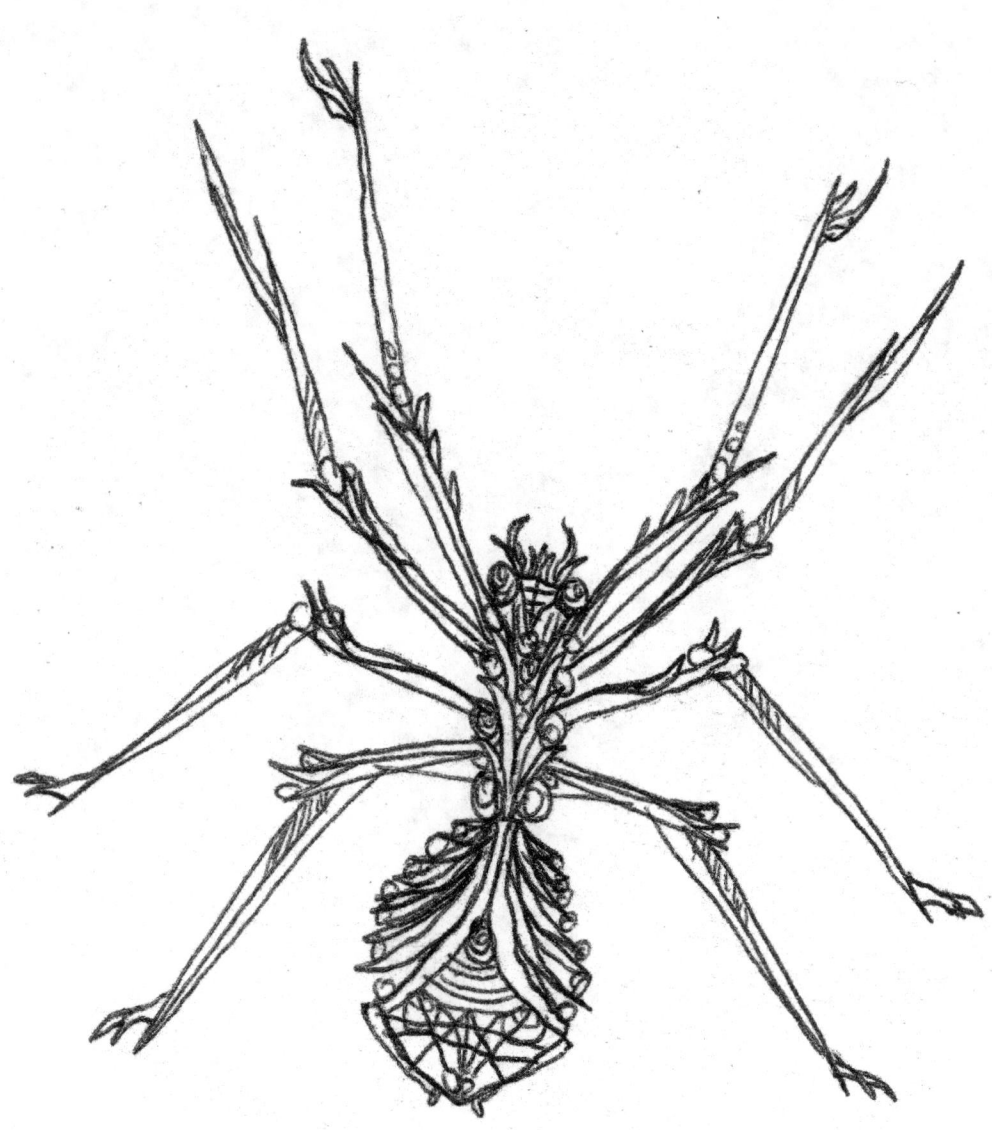

Grapnel

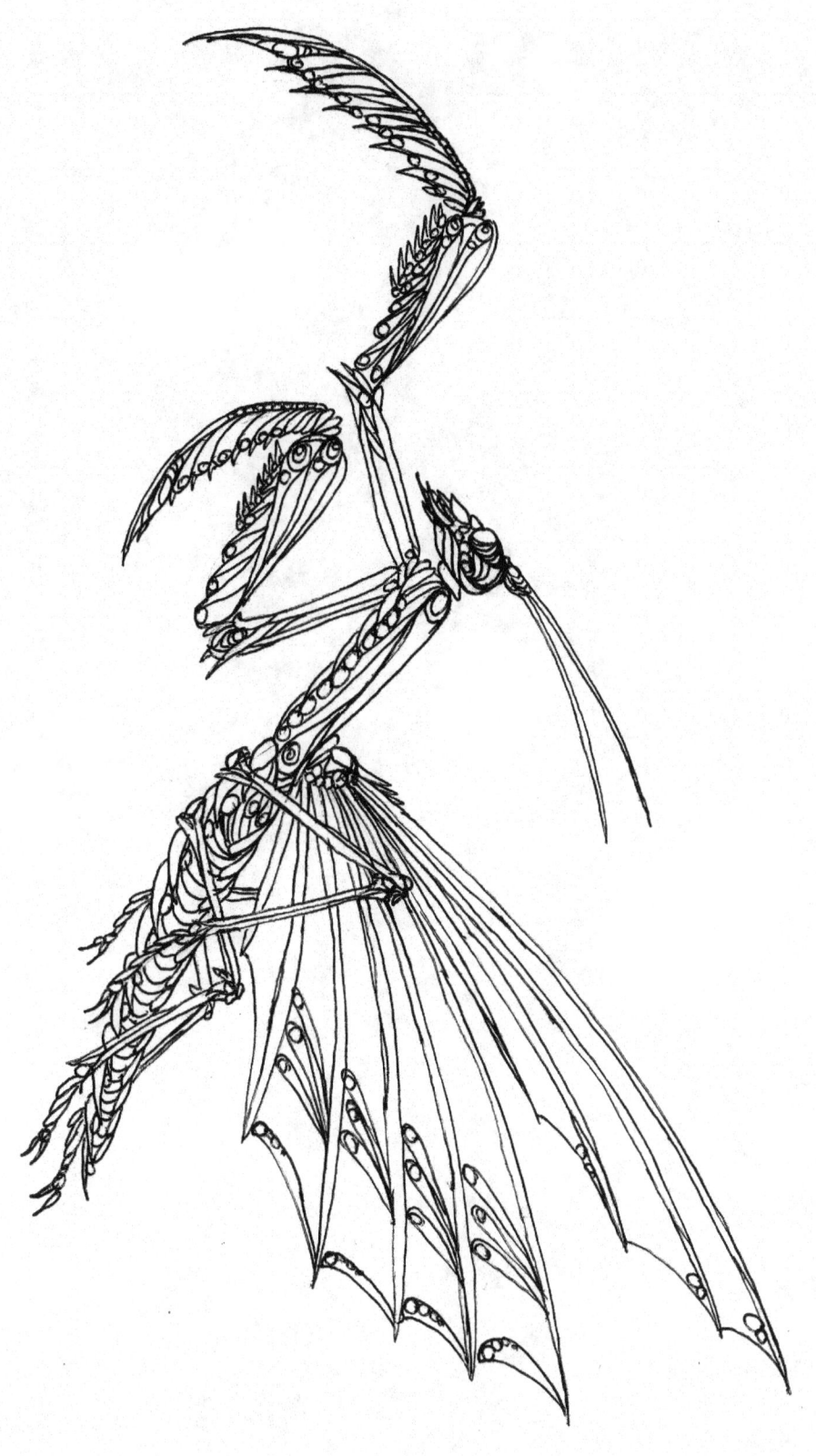

Breeze

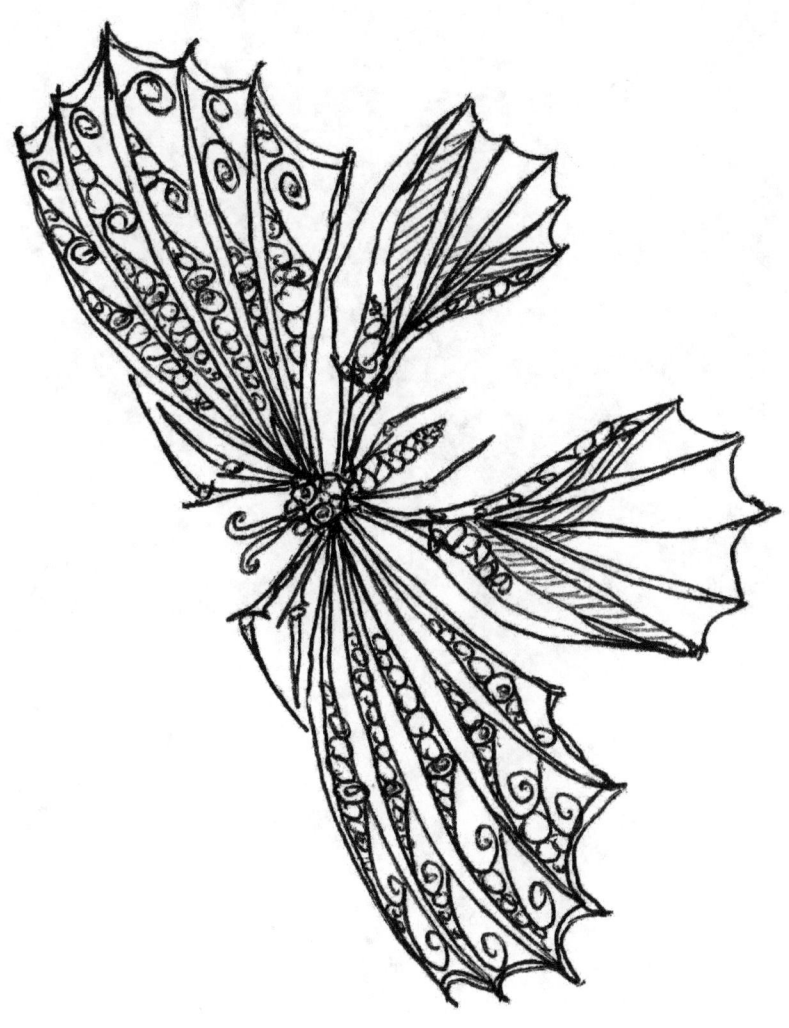

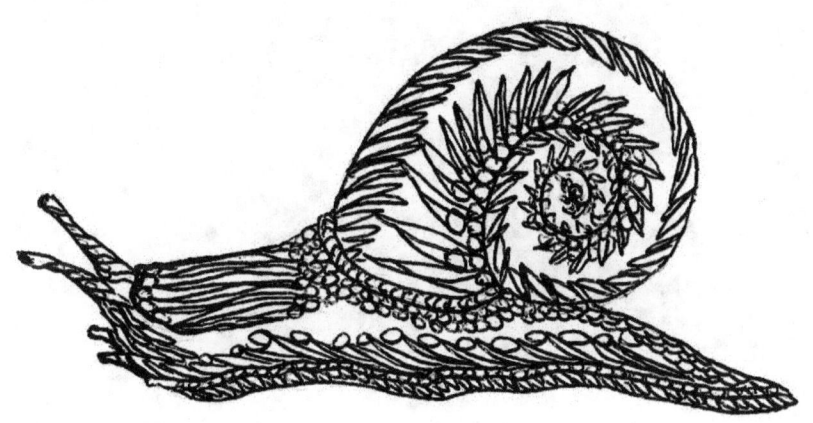

Fang

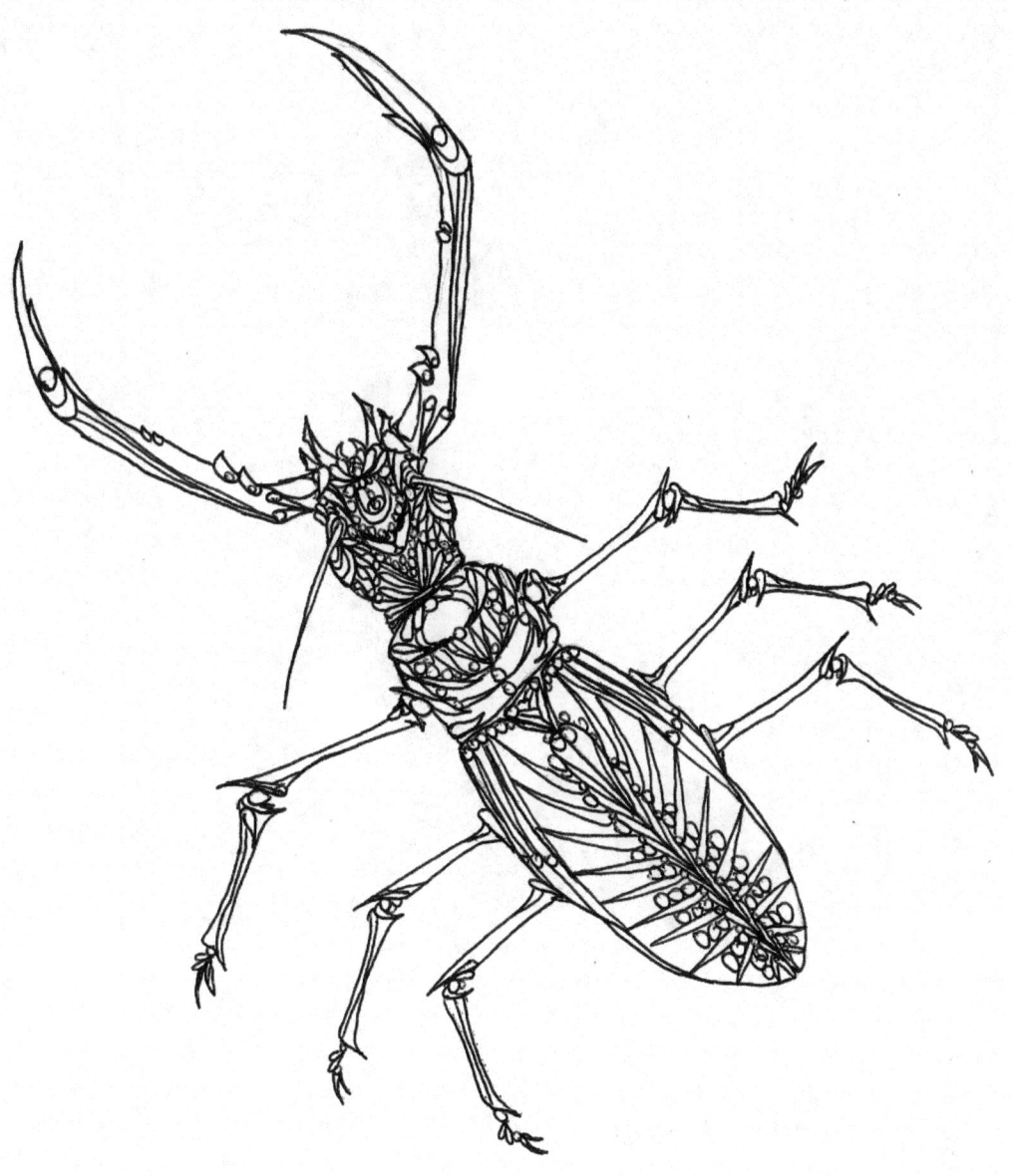

The Realm of the Fantastic

Shard

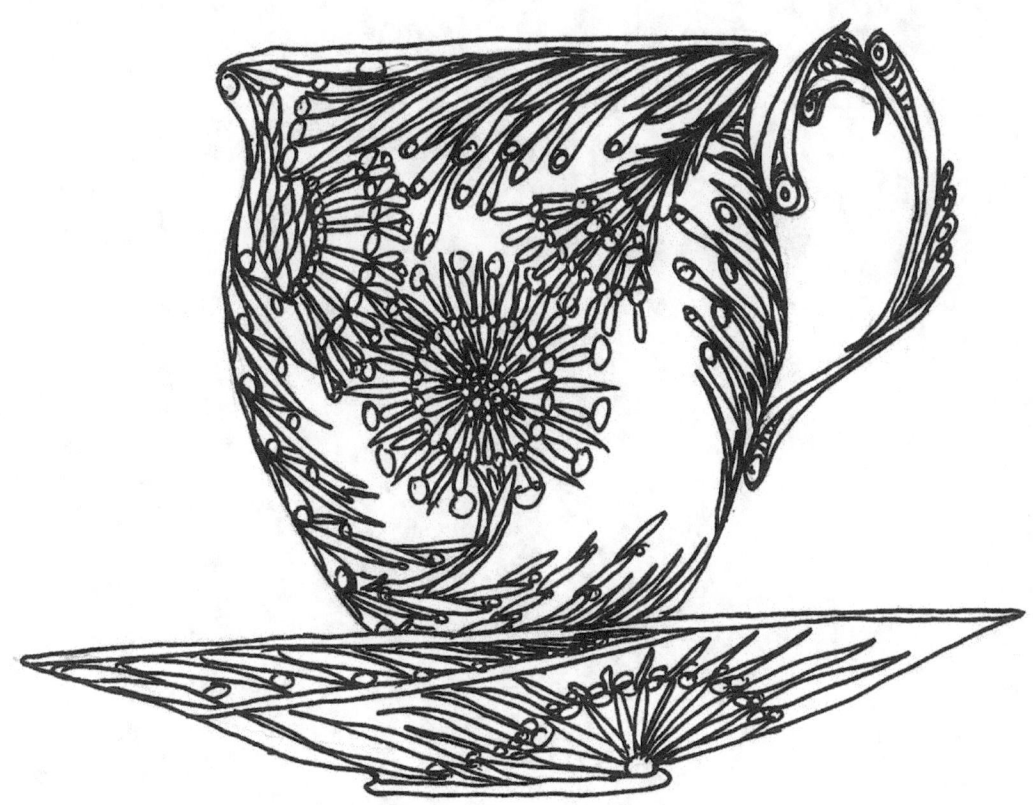

Hands

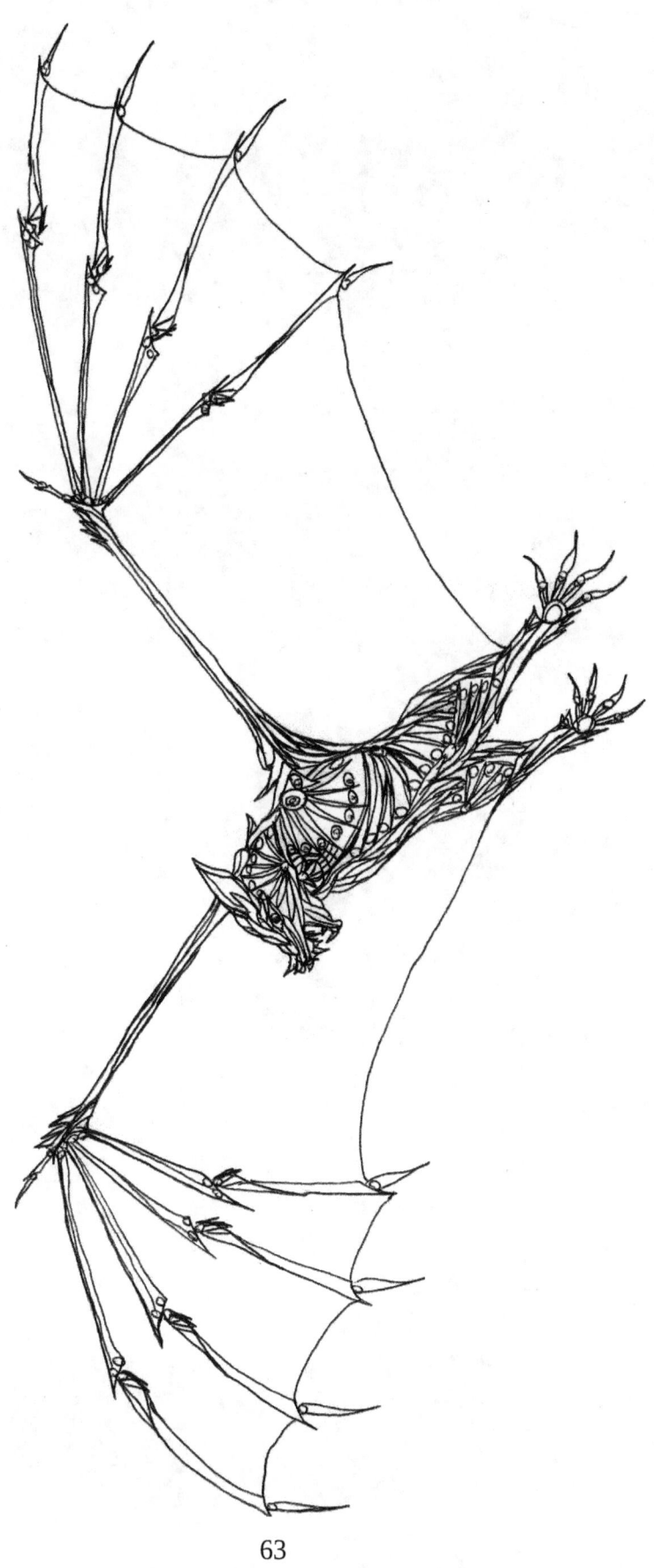

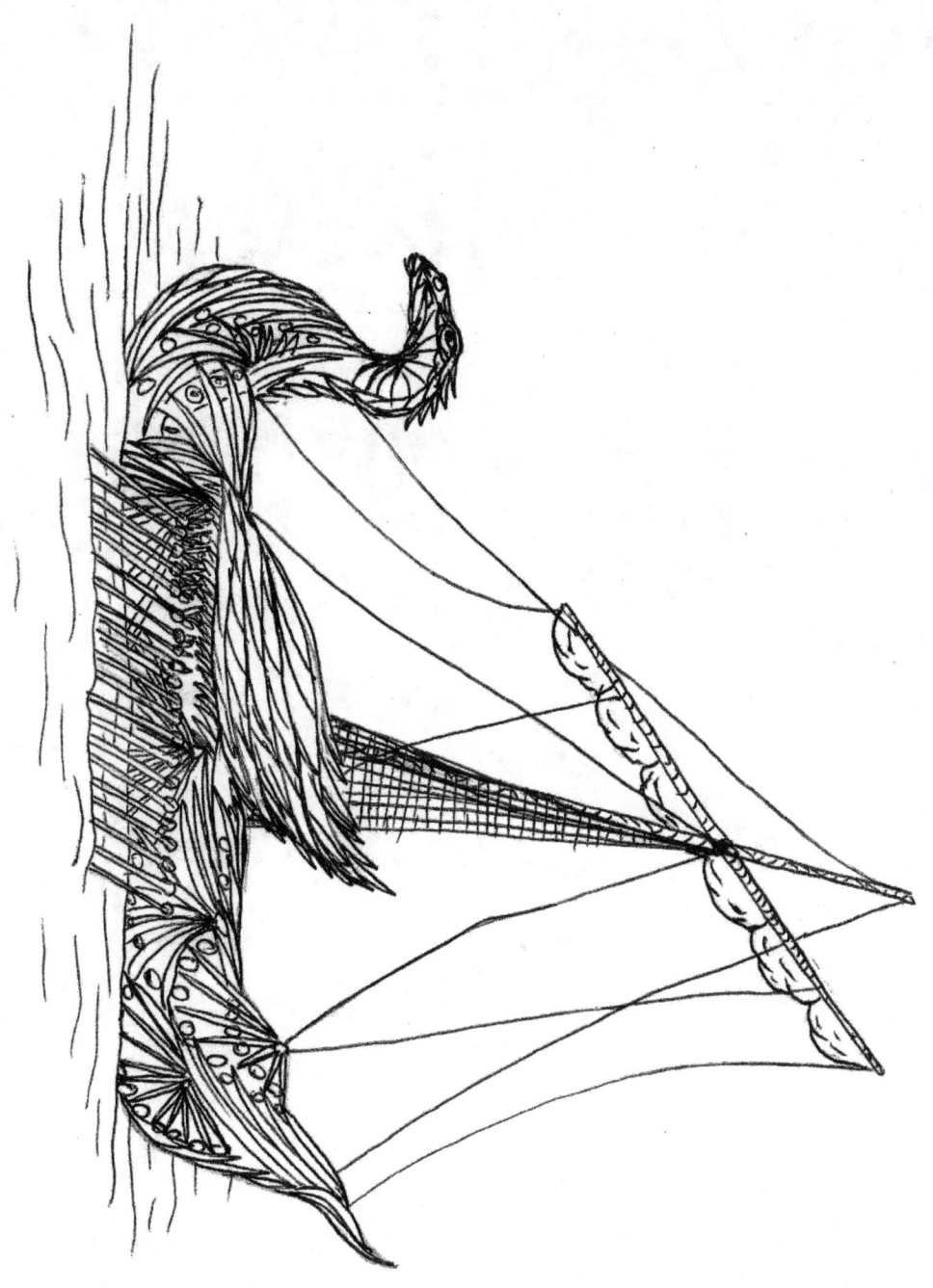

My Hand

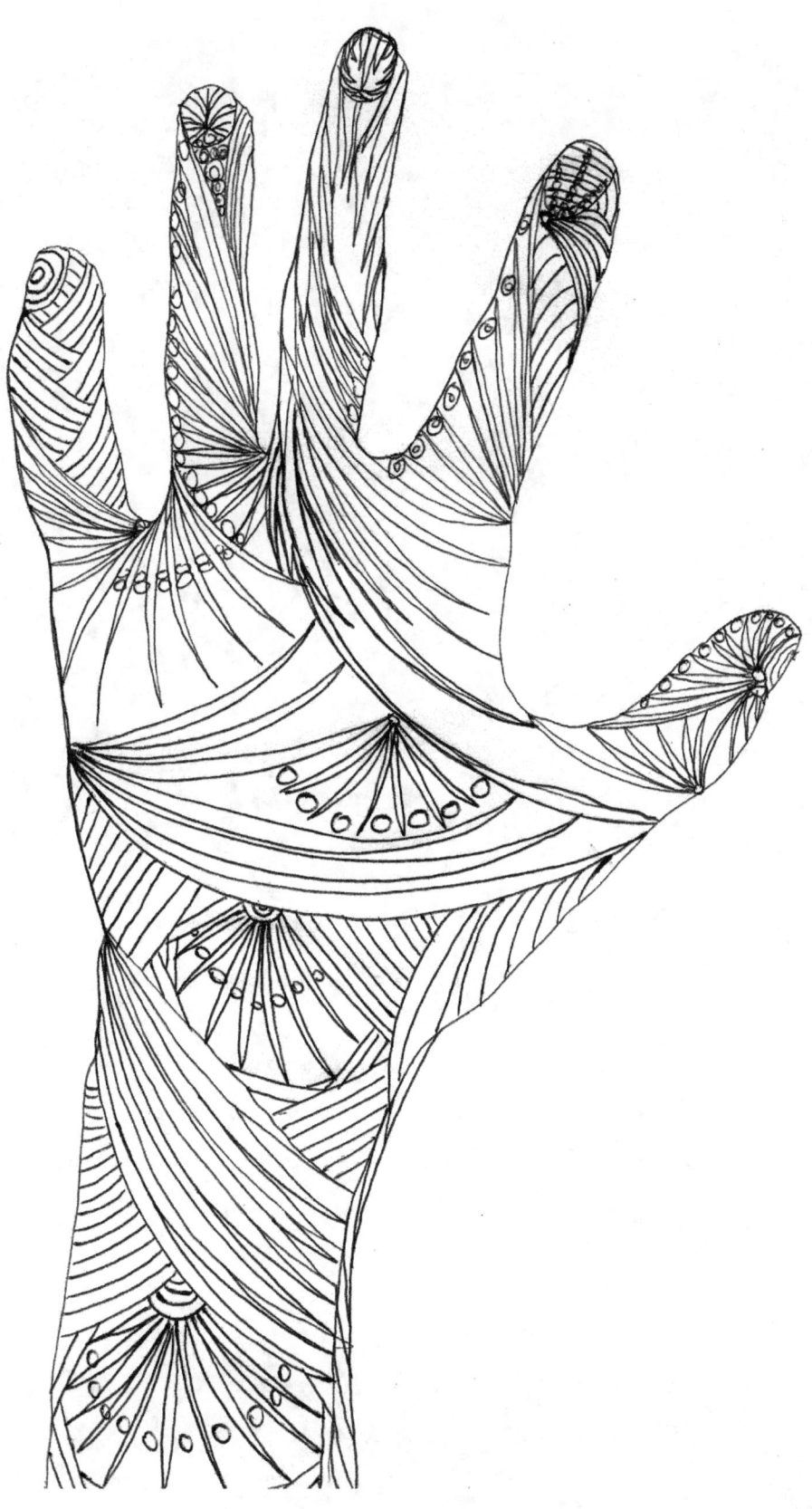

Hunger

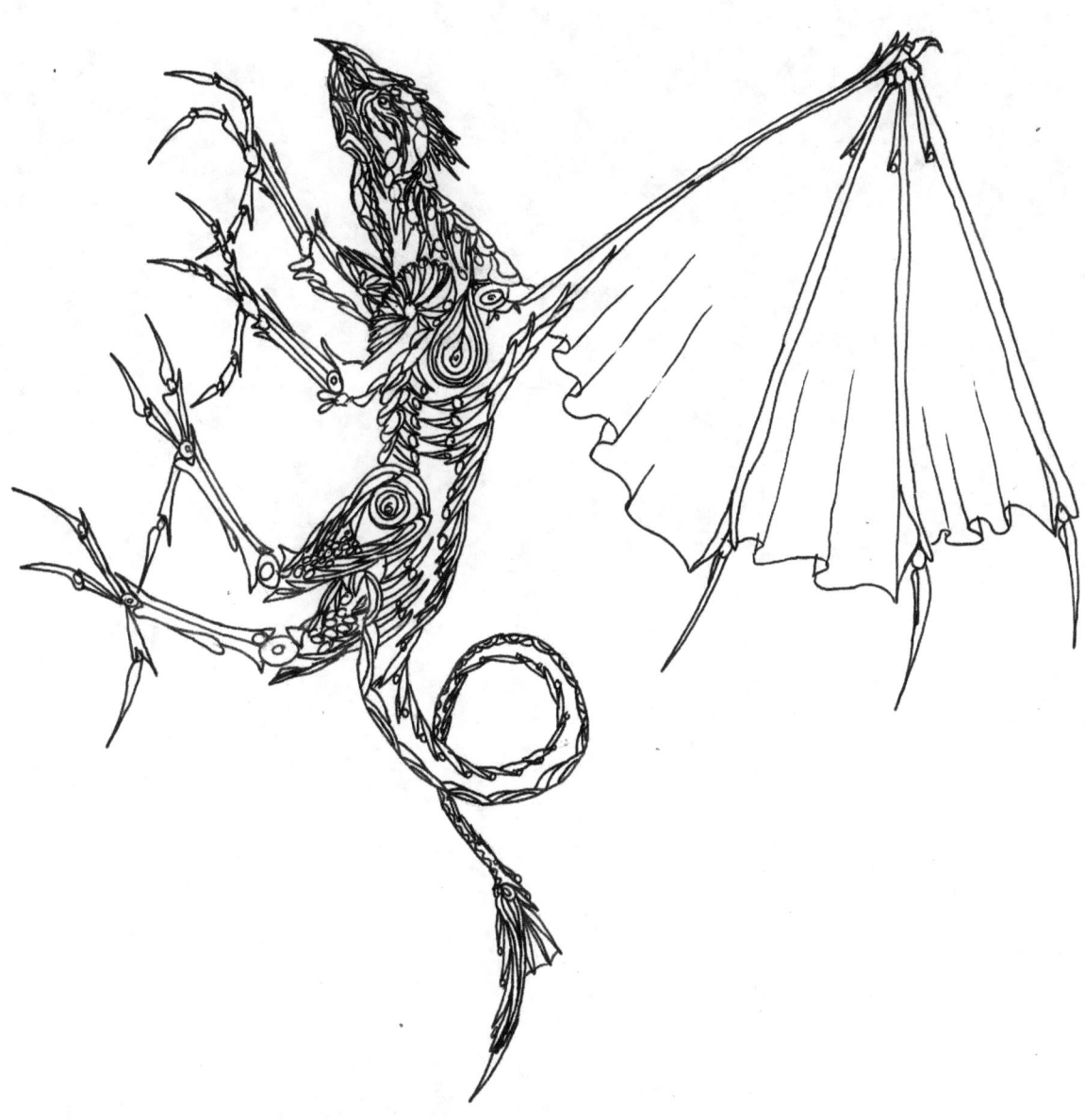

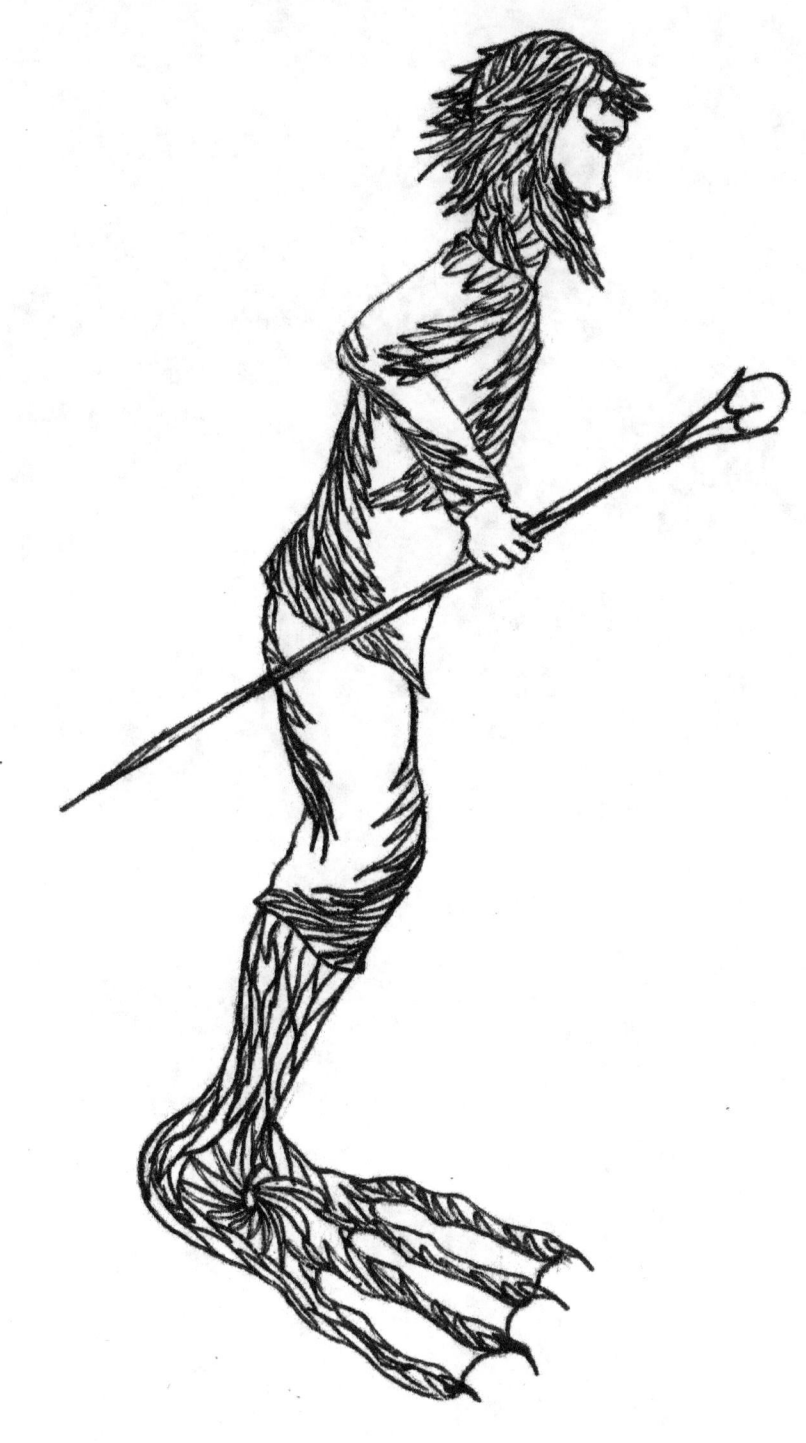

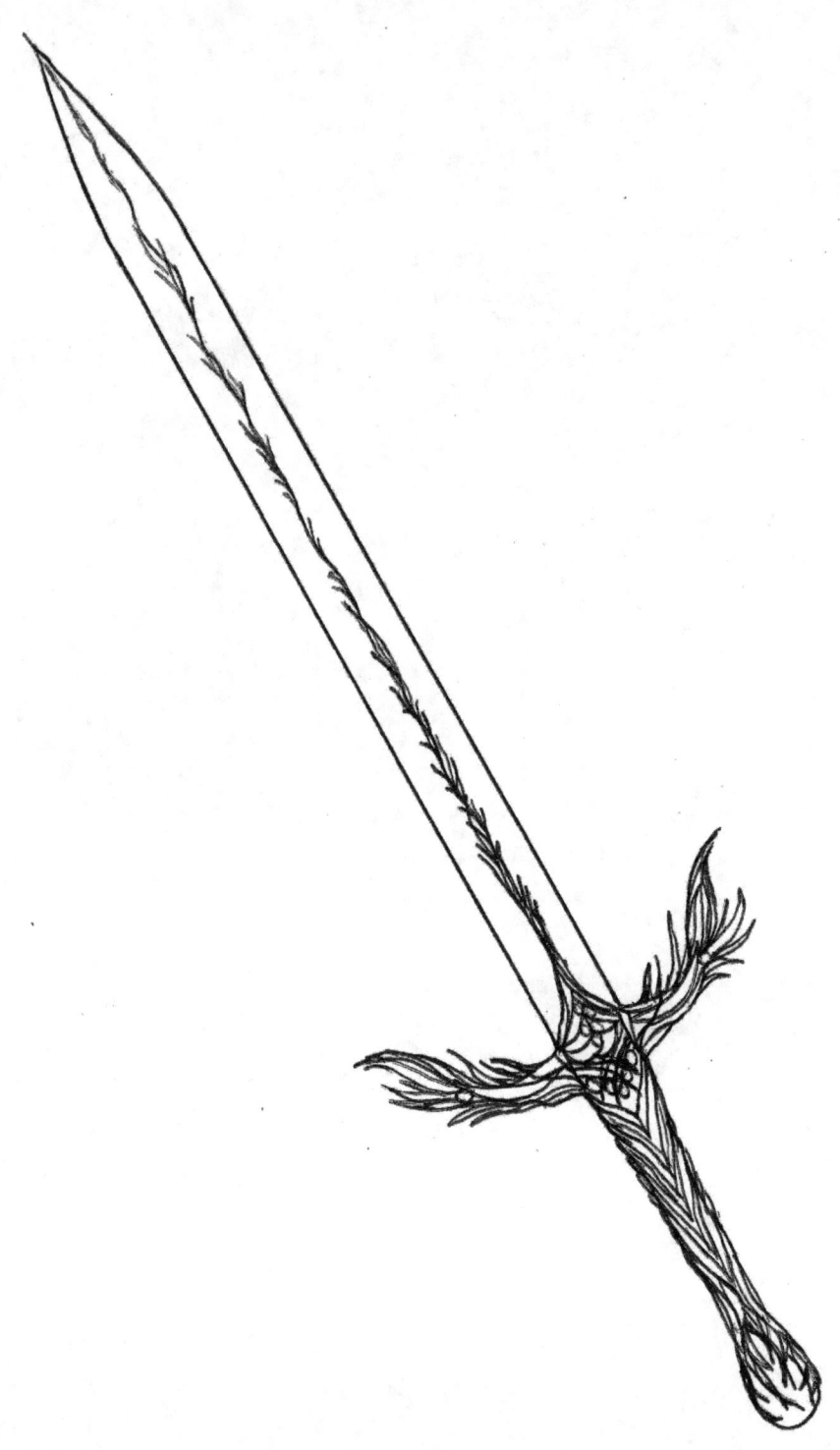

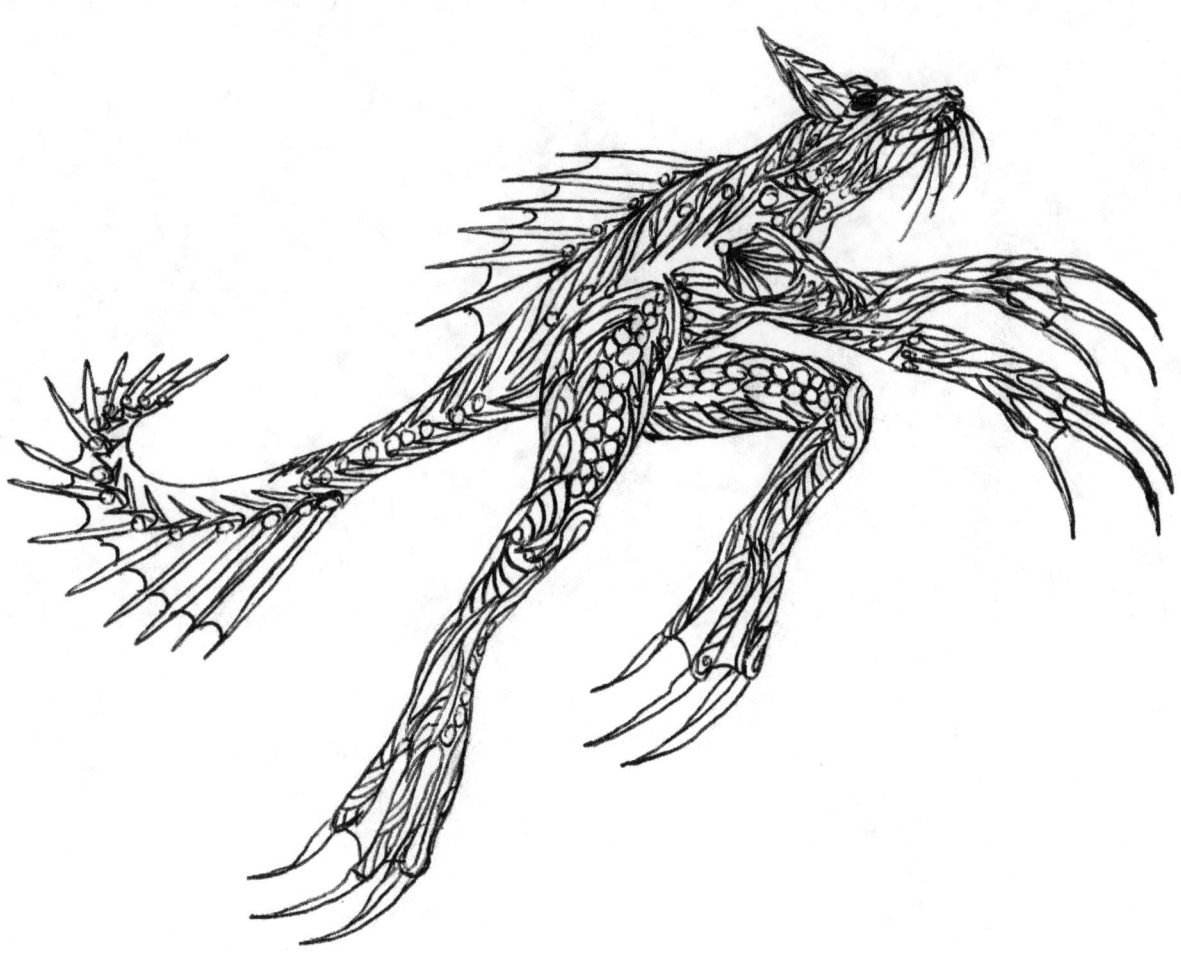

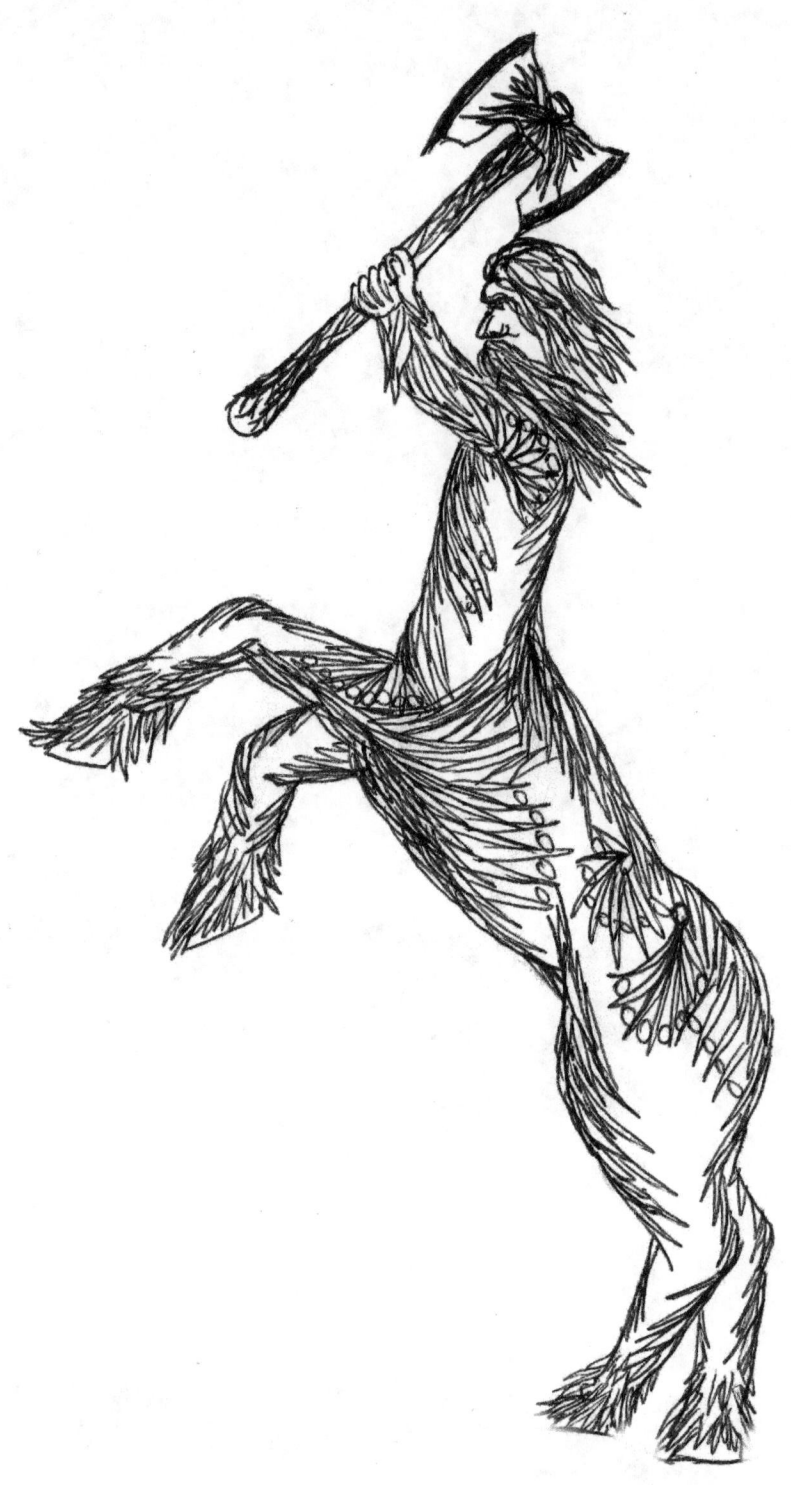

Wind

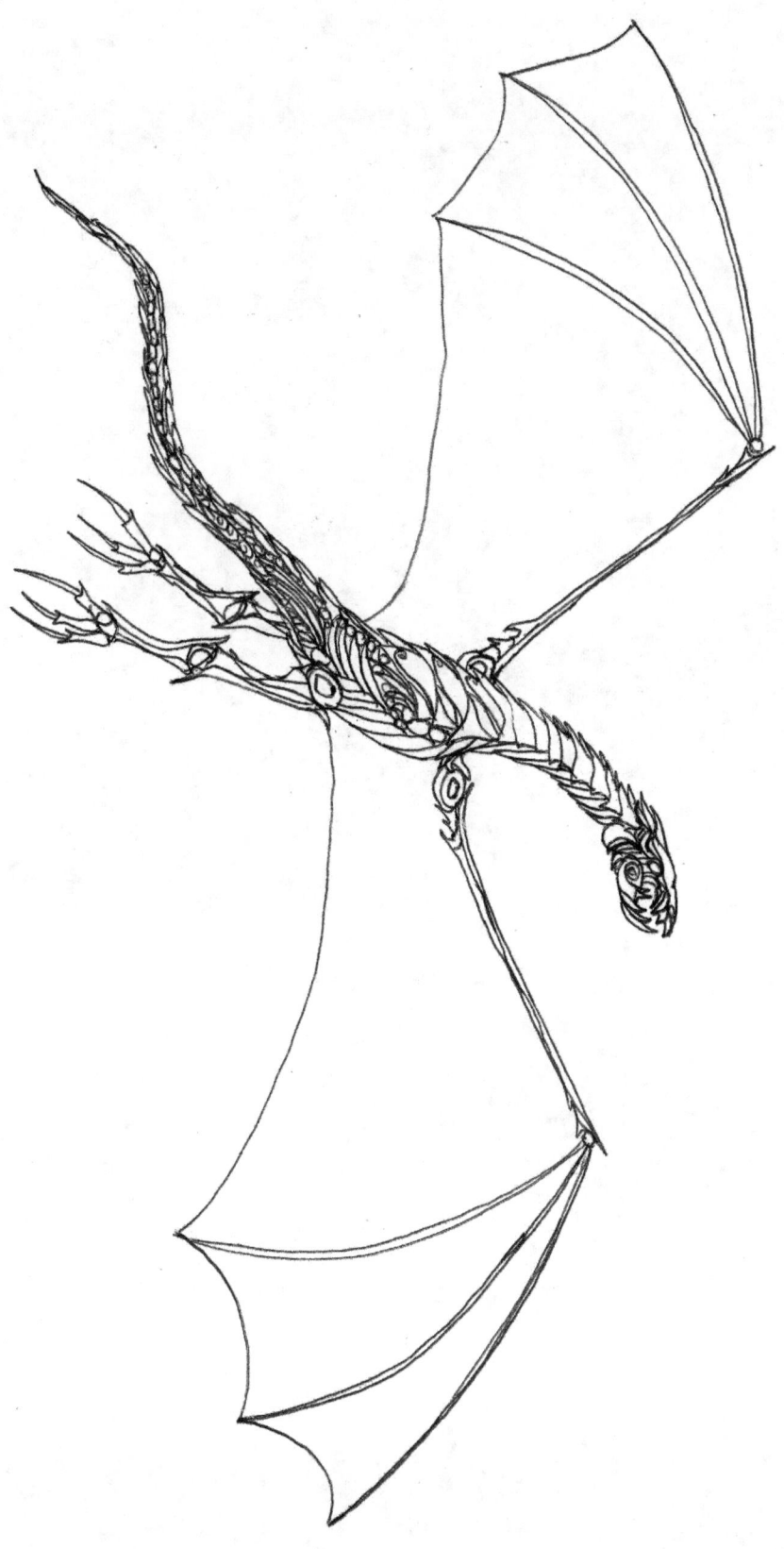

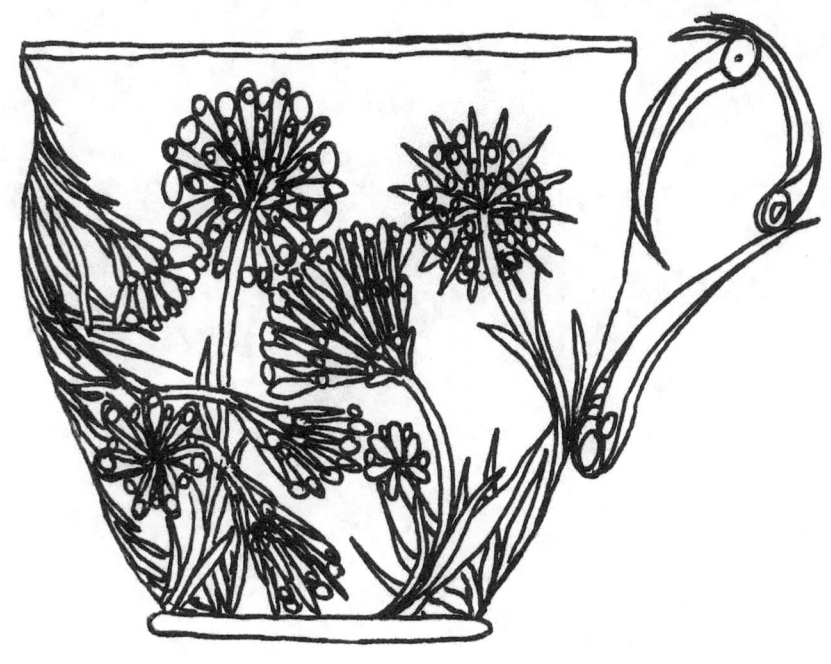

Fare thee well,
till another time.

www.ingramcontent.com/pod-product-compliance
Lightning Source LLC
Chambersburg PA
CBHW081120180526
45170CB00008B/2932